RELIGION, POLITICS, AND OIL

RELIGION, POLITICS, AND OIL

THE VOLATILE MIX IN THE MIDDLE EAST

Charles A. Kimball

ABINGDON PRESS
Nashville

RELIGION, POLITICS, AND OIL
THE VOLATILE MIX IN THE MIDDLE EAST

Copyright © 1992 by Abingdon Press.

Library of Congress Cataloging-in-Publication Data

Kimball, Charles.
    Religion, politics, and oil: the volatile mix in the middle east. / Charles A. Kimball.
      p.   cm.
    Includes bibliographical references
    ISBN 0-687-35973-2
    1.Middle East—Politics and Government—1945–   2.Persian Gulf War, 1991—Religious aspects.   I. Title.
    DS63.1.K55   1992   91-47140
    956—dc20   CIP

ISBN 0-687-35973-2

All quotations from Scripture are from the New Revised Standard Version Bible, copyright © 1989, by the Division of Christian Education of the National Council of the Churches of Christ in the U.S.A. Used by permission.

Printed in the United States of America on recycled, acid-free paper.

CONTENTS

For Sarah and Elliot

ACKNOWLEDGMENTS

The Gulf crisis altered the political map of the Middle East even as it illustrated some of the systemic problems plaguing this region. The crisis and war also brought to the surface a variety of religious, political, and economic concerns that affect all of us who share this planet. The present text explores these factors in the context of our heightened awareness informed by these traumatic events.

When the crisis in the Gulf erupted onto the world stage, I was preparing another book related to the contemporary Middle East. That book, *Angle of Vision: Christians and the Middle East*, is the principle text used in a variety of churches during the 1992 ecumenical study on the Middle East. The text focuses on the history of Christianity in the holy lands as well as the various ways North American Christians are linked with the Middle Eastern Christians today. It explores the challenges and opportunities for mutuality in witness, service, education, and public policy advocacy ministries.

The two books converge at some points of political analysis and learnings from the Gulf war. Both texts draw upon previously published articles though they differ in the respective ways the political analysis and examples connect with the major foci of each book. Readers of this present text may wish to explore the themes of mission, service, education and advocacy as these are developed in *Angle of Vision*.

A portion of chapter 1 below, "Religion," is a modified version of material published previously in *Striving Together: A Way Forward in Christian-Muslim Relations*. I am grateful to Orbis Books for permission to incorporate several pages from my book into this present text.

Religion, Politics, and Oil grows out of a longstanding and direct involvement with Middle East issues. A wide variety of unnamed people—religious and political leaders, journalists, academics, relief workers, taxi drivers, et al.—have helped shape and modify my views. The engagement with various individuals and among groups where I've made presentations intensified during and after the Gulf war. This dynamic process has been critical in helping me refine and articulate perspectives. I wish to express particular appreciation to Catherine Essoyan for her critical insights and suggestions concerning drafts of this text. Rex Matthews and Bob Ratcliff of Abingdon Press have offered invaluable editorial guidance during the process of shaping and producing the book.

Writing a book—even a short one—is often a family affair. Writing during this past year has been especially challenging in view of the heavy public speaking, media interviews, and other demands on people with Middle East expertise. My spouse, Nancy, and our children, Sarah and Elliot, have been remarkably supportive. This book is dedicated to our children in the hope that they and their children one day will inhabit a less volatile world than the one we see through the lens of the Gulf crisis and war.

FOREWORD

The expertise and courage of Charles Kimball first came to my attention as we met at the Iranian embassy in Washington, D.C. to prepare for a visit to a country in turmoil. We were traveling to Iran to bring a Christmas message of peace to the Ayatollah Khomeini. It was December 1979, and America was enraged by the hostage crisis.

As Charles briefed us on the plane, in the hotel in Tehran, and on the road to Ghom, I was distressed to discover how little I knew about Islam and the Middle East. Why was Iran collapsing into chaos? Why did they call America "the Great Satan"? Did we contribute to the nervous breakdown of a nation?

As we talked with the Ayatollah and other religious leaders, the militant students, and noted international scholars, a picture began to emerge. We had put the Shah into power in a CIA coup, subjecting the people of Iran to twenty-five years of brutal tyranny. We had participated in the militarization of this society, pouring in billions of dollars of modern arms until Iran sank under the weight of its dinosaur armor. We had participated in the ruination of their agriculture in the name of "development," forcing five million people from the villages into urban slums. Again in the name of "development," multinational corporations built assembly plants, putting the poor to work at low wages and repatriating the profits out of the country.

The American people knew none of this. We were being taught that Iran was a nation of dangerous, crazy people. Traveling with Charles through the streets of Tehran, we met dozens of friendly people, many of whom had studied in America. They looked upon the American people as charming, dedicated to democracy, reasonable, and friendly. Again and again they asked, "How did the American people lose control of their foreign policy? How could you allow your leaders to export dictatorship and economic exploitation?" In a meeting with professors from the Teheran universities, we received one answer. They said, "As we came to know the American people, we discovered that few of them bother to *read*. They come home tired, listen to a few minutes of TV news, then switch to the sit-coms."

During the months of the hostage crisis, those of us who had observed the Iranian revolution from within were asked to speak all around the country. The moment the hostages came home, such interest in the Middle East abruptly ceased. Once again, the fickle attention span of the American people prevented the learning of lessons needed to influence future foreign policy.

When the Gulf war struck, we were unprepared yet again. We had no fund of information to prepare us to make balanced judgments. As Charles points out, the media available to most of us do not serve us well. In a time of international crisis, TV images are more likely to inflame the emotions than inform the mind. As the camera turns to images of conflict, the dehumanizing enemy-making processes proceed apace. Rhetorical flourishes of demagogues sap the nerve of public support for peaceful solutions. Once the war begins, it feeds on its own brutal logic. Suddenly everyone is expected to "support the troops." Managed news guarantees that, once again, truth is the first casualty of war, and compassion is the second. Analyses are superficial and seldom contextualized. "Sound-byte" communications can stampede even a sophisticated people if they are not globally aware and informed.

Charles Kimball believes this is a teachable moment. He is convinced that committed Christians, once informed, can become a powerful force to influence the course of history. He is well equipped by experience and advanced study to guide us along such a journey of understanding.

Charles raises critical questions which can be summarized by a simple statement: armies may win wars, but they cannot bring peace to the world. The most "just" of all imaginable wars cannot of itself secure a just peace.

We will lose the peace if we succumb to a heady triumphalism, if we surrender to the militarism which can run so rampant among us. We will win if we at last perceive the utter futility of seeking security in the Middle East (or anywhere else) by militarizing the region. The universal consensus among religious as well as political leaders was that Saddam Hussein had to be contained. His cancerous influence had to be combatted by sanctions designed to paralyze his capacity to remain in Kuwait and to menace his neighbors.

We must not forget, however, that we participated in the creation of this monstrous military machine in Iraq. In many respects we are seeing the last gasps of the Nixon Doctrine, which was built on the premise that if we armed client states in regions we wished to control, they would fight our wars for us. We could project power without the threat of body bags returning to the United States to alienate American public opinion. Following this reasoning, we poured billions of dollars of modern arms into Iran, while the Soviet Union was arming its client state, Iraq. With the ascension of Iranian nationalism, our puppet regime suddenly asserted a mind of its own; the robot turned against its master.

So we tilted toward Iraq as our new client state, pressed into service to punish our old one. The CIA offered logistical support for the Iraqi invasion of Iran. France, Germany, Britain, China, even little Switzerland rushed to the lucrative arms trade with Iraq. We provided $5 billion in food, making Iraq one of the top beneficiaries of U.S. taxpayer-financed foodstuffs in the 1980s. Saddam was able to concentrate his dwindling cash reserves on his war with Iran and his military build-up. Up until a week before the invasion of Kuwait, the administration vigorously opposed congressional action to suspend United States Department of Agriculture subsidies to Iraq. This occurred in spite of Iraq's horrendous human rights abuses and even its use of chemical weapons against its own people.

We in the U.S. must take care to learn the lessons of this first test of post-Cold War diplomacy, to sort out the root causes of the ongoing difficulties in the Middle East. We will lose the peace if we continue to believe that war and the militarization of the region is necessary to perpetuate the industrial countries' addiction to cheap oil. If we factor in the horrendous military costs of protecting our oil supply, we will discover that imported oil is now far more expensive than any number of alternative, renewable forms of energy.

> The end of the fossil fuel age is now in sight. As the world lurches from one energy crisis to another, fossil fuel dependence threatens at every turn to derail the global economy or disrupt its environmental support systems. If we are to ensure a healthy and prosperous world for future generations, only a few decades remain to redirect the energy economy.[1]

We must develop a far different energy system. We were off to a good start in the 1970s, but we dropped the ball. Fortunately, the "elements of an energy system that would be truly sustainable are now available to us."[2] Renewable energy from the sun is already competitive in price, and could supply 70% of our energy needs within 40 years.

We will lose the peace if we fall victim to the capacity of modern warfare to cauterize our finer sensibilities, to blunt our sense of common humanity, and to brutalize the mentality and spirit of our young, who are increasingly desensitized to the horror of institutionalized mayhem. In the process of brutalizing others, we brutalize ourselves.

The dehumanizing enemy-making process takes over our minds all to easily. Too few words were spoken in the media during the Gulf war to express empathy with the Iraqi families suffering so terribly and living with terror every day. A California state legislator who emigrated from Iraq shook his colleagues when he rose to say, "I am a loyal American. I have no doubt that

---

1. Christopher Flavin and Nicholas Lenssen, *Beyond the Petroleum Age* (Washington: World Watch Institute, 1990), p. 5.
2. Ibid.

we had to contain Saddam. But will you please grieve with me as my heart bleeds for my relatives and friends in that tragic nation?"

Arab-bashing is all the more destructive of our spiritual integrity as it grows virtually unchallenged by even the brightest and best among us. Charles Kimball points out that Christians and Muslims make up half the world's population. We simply must find ways to cooperate in mutual understanding. This book is a giant step in bringing that hope to realization.

The Reverend C. Dale White
Resident Bishop
New York Annual Conference
The United Methodist Church

INTRODUCTION

There has been an attack . . . bombs are now hitting the center of the city. War has begun in Baghdad. (John Holliman, CNN reporter in Baghdad, Jan. 16, 1991)

The nation is at war—a war that should have been avoided. And a great human tragedy of yet unknown proportions has begun to unfold . . . We opposed the war on moral grounds and remain opposed to it now . . . . (From "A Call to the Churches" issued by more than 100 prominent U.S. church leaders, February 13, 1991)

As he (Jesus) came near and saw the city, he wept over it, saying, "If you, even you, had only recognized on this day the things that make for peace! But now they are hidden from your eyes." (Luke 19:41–42)

On January 16, 1991, less than 24 hours after the United Nations' deadline for the Iraqi withdrawal from Kuwait, the United States-led military forces launched a massive air assault on targets in Iraq and Kuwait. That day is now firmly fixed in the minds of millions of Americans who sat stunned and mesmerized in front of televisions while reports of the war began flooding the airwaves. For the first time, a major conflict was covered live via satellite—including reports from Cable News Network (CNN) journalists observing the heavy bombardment of Baghdad from their hotel room window. Some commentators later dubbed this clash the first high-tech "living room" war.

The war with Iraq captured and sustained the attention of the public unlike any event since the seizure and holding of U.S. diplomats as hostages in Iran a decade earlier. In the first few days of the conflict, the major networks provided round-the-clock coverage. In subsequent weeks the barrage of information continued as hundreds of correspondents provided details, conveyed images, and reported on developments in the unfolding drama. Working under the severe limitations of strict review and censorship imposed by all the governments involved, journalists sought information and new angles on the events dominating the world stage. The kaleidoscope of details emanating from TV, radio, and print media served both to clarify certain issues and confuse others in this multi-faceted and convoluted affair.

Conflicting images characterized the U.S. domestic scene. While virtually everyone expressed support for the men and women who were serving in the military, and opinion polls consistently indicated strong support for the policies of the Bush Administration, many people also expressed confusion, anxiety, and serious misgivings in the face of overwhelming and often disconnected pieces of information. Saddam Hussein's brutal tyranny and aggression seemed obvious, but that was clearly not the whole picture. The world has no shortage of ruthless dictators with unwarranted illusions of grandeur and sickening records of human rights abuses. Nagging questions kept surfacing: How exactly did we get into the mess? Why had the U.S. and other Western powers supported Iraq until August of 1990? Had all the diplomatic and political avenues been exhausted? Why would large masses of people—from Morocco to Indonesia—take to the streets to protest the Allied military offensive? Was it necessary to obliterate the Iraqi infrastructure in order to liberate Kuwait? How many innocent civilians were being hurt? What were the longer term consequences of such massive damage?

Having spoken on Middle East issues at a wide variety of public gatherings—from church and civic groups to university and business communities—during late 1990 and the first half of 1991, I can attest to this widespread confusion and ambiguity. Opinion polls failed to reflect the persistent concerns of large numbers of people who frequently remained silent for fear of being perceived

16

or branded as unpatriotic or unsupportive of Allied troops. For many, the horror of war, however justified, was not obscured by enthusiastic and simplistic language depicting this confrontation in terms reminiscent of the Super Bowl.

The world watched for six weeks as wrenching human tragedies were conveyed starkly through the unblinking eye of the TV camera: the physical destruction resulting from more than 103,000 Allied sorties (most of which were bombing missions), SCUD missile attacks on civilian targets, environmental terrorism, and the pathetic surrender of tens of thousands of beleaguered Iraqi soldiers, many of whom were poorly trained conscripts unsure as to why they were there and what they were supposed to be fighting for.

In the months following the war, the plight of several million Iraqi citizens came shockingly into view. In addition to enormous problems caused by the severe damage to Iraq's infrastructure, thousands of Kurdish people in the North and Shi'ite Muslims in the South of Iraq were crushed by the remnant of Saddam Hussein's military. These Iraqis made the mistake of heeding President Bush's unambiguous call to "rise up and overthrow the dictator Saddam." When it became clear that these insurgent groups would not receive military assistance from the Allied forces, their dream of toppling Hussein's regime turned quickly into a nightmare. The "lucky" ones were those who those who left their homes and belongings to flee into an uncertain future as refugees. Thousands more perished before international efforts to provide humanitarian assistance began to reach the hapless refugees.

The war stimulated widespread debate about the short and long-term political consequences for the region. The various reactions visibly rippled through the world community like aftershocks from a massive earthquake. As the military outcome became certain, an ever-growing circle of political leaders and analysts voiced their views that this war would have major political, religious, and economic repercussions for years, perhaps decades, to come: Some were optimistic; most were guarded; many feared that the war would complicate further the search for solutions to daunting regional issues.

The trauma of the war combined with a keen awareness that many of the relevant issues would continue to demand attention long after the cessation of fighting prompted Abingdon Press to develop a series of resources for use in the churches. When Abingdon officials first asked me to prepare this text, I was hesitant. The various issues raised by the war defy simple analysis and easy resolution. In addition, most people are anything but dispassionate: popular images and perceptions are laced with highly charged emotions. Even so, in the course of our conversations it became increasingly clear that such a resource could be valuable. Months after the full-scale fighting stopped, numerous ambiguities remain throughout the troubled Middle East. While the answers do not come easily, it is hoped that this book will help sharpen the focus on some of the right questions. People of faith and concerned citizens must endeavor to understand the issues if they hope to work constructively toward the most positive future feasible. We trust this effort will contribute toward the process.

Our purpose in this text is to provide a framework for understanding major elements that are and will continue to be important in this vital and often confusing part of the world. By examining religious, political, and economic factors shaping the Middle East landscape, we hope to encourage a more critical and nuanced appreciation for these interrelated dimensions. This, in turn, should facilitate understanding and interpretation of the unfolding events as well as encourage more thoughtful and responsible approaches to an array of vexing and volatile problems.

The principle audience here addressed is the Christian community in the West. The churches have a crucial role to play, both in the society at large and in relation to Middle East conflicts in particular. That role, informed by deep moral and spiritual concerns, must be defined through a process of honest engagement with the issues. Although Christians do not agree on what precisely it is that faith requires in a given situation, most agree on the importance of a pastoral, reconciling, and prophetic role in society. The life of faith cannot and should not be separated from public policy issues.

The importance of the Middle East imposes a responsibility for prudent and persevering action. U.S. citizens bear a special burden since the actions of our government—be they constructive or detrimental—directly impinge on the lives of people in the Middle East. The attitudes and actions of U.S. Christians can help shape public policy debates within our society. Our active involvement could make the difference between the achievement of peace with justice or continuing conflict.

Many prominent church leaders and institutional bodies were visibly active in the months prior to, during, and immediately after the six weeks of hostilities. Virtually all agreed on the cruelty of Saddam Hussein's aggression and the need to halt and reverse it. Their questions centered not on whether, but on how to do so. Prominent Christian voices were audible at points all along the political spectrum.

On one extreme, religious broadcasting stations featured a host of TV preachers poised in front of enormous American flags—the size normally reserved for display by imported car dealers. With this imposing backdrop, the TV preachers offered seemingly uncritical support for any and all U.S. policy decisions. The line between church and state was practically non-existent. One can only imagine how such an admixture must have appeared to Asian, African, Latin American, or Middle Eastern Christians.

Many evangelical and fundamentalist Christians focused primarily on Armageddon scenarios, concentrating their energies on piecing together the puzzle of a premillennial theological framework. If book sales and radio talk shows are indicative, several million U.S. Christians were absorbed in a tedious effort to interpret tidbits of news as indicators that the final showdown at Armageddon was imminent. Quite apart from this approach to biblical prophecy, some Americans identified doomsday scenarios in which the Gulf crisis might be the spark igniting a wider conflagration.

To a surprising degree, however, a large number of Protestant, Orthodox, and Catholic leaders took a different approach: they were visibly united in their opposition to the massive military buildup and the prosecution of the war. Their positions were often strong and sometimes controversial, particularly in view of the popular support for the war in the general public. Writing at the end of 1991, James Wall, Editor of *The Christian Century*, cited these and other "religious dimensions" that made the war in the Gulf the "top religion story" of the year:

> For religious people especially the war and the long prelude to it fostered an intense debate over some large moral challenges. The Kuwaiti crisis presented questions about Christian-Jewish-Muslim relations, about justice and peace between Jews and Arabs, about the place of Islam in the modern world, about the history of Western involvement in the region, and —far from least—about the morality of war.[1]

In the aftermath of the war, the minority views espoused by many U.S. Christian leaders continue to reverberate in church circles and in the larger society. Now that the actual combat has long since subsided, the parades and victory celebrations are over, and attention has shifted to wider regional issues, a less emotional assessment of their major arguments is possible—and useful. The various concerns emanating from a wide spectrum of representative church leaders and governing bodies provide much needed perspective for understanding important dimensions of the conflict. This, in turn, can move us toward a more coherent and constructive approach to the multitude of problems that inevitably will surface in the Middle East.

Why did so many church leaders oppose the war? Several different and sometimes interrelated concerns were visible in the various public pronouncements and actions. First, many in the churches raised a fundamental moral objection to armed conflict as an acceptable basis for resolving conflicts. The pacifist position, embraced almost universally in the early church, continues to inform the thinking of the historic peace churches (Mennonites, Brethren, and Quakers) as well as many within the Roman Catholic Church and different Protestant communions. These Christians seek to emulate the examples of Jesus, Martin Luther King, Jr., even Mahatma Gandhi, as they pursue nonviolent—not passive—means of addressing injustice and resolving conflicts. In the tradition of these spiritual leaders, scores of Christians committed themselves to prayer, fasting, and other expressions of spiritual

---

1. James M. Wall, "War, Sex, Dissension: Religion Stories of 1991," *The Christian Century* (Dec. 18–25, 1991), p. 1187.

discipline even as they engaged in education and public policy advocacy initiatives.

Other Christians, less certain of a pacifist stance, argued on moral and pragmatic grounds: violence begets violence. They employed the same arguments for seeking diplomatic and political means (including boycotts and sanctions) that have been commonly offered for years in relation to the conflict in South Africa. Why, they asked, was it necessary for the U.S. and others to resort to military options so quickly in this case? The fact that the Allied forces were successful militarily does not prove that this was the only or the best way to deal with the Iraqi aggression. Many feared that middle and long-term consequences of a military victory would only complicate and exacerbate already precarious regional dynamics. The rapid decision to pursue military options will be revisited in analyses for years to come, particularly given the ambiguous signals and communications between Washington and Baghdad just prior to the invasion on August 2, 1990.

Many suggested that the goal of durable peace and stability was not likely to be secured through war. A survey of Middle East history in the twentieth century underscores the point. Some short term goals may be satisfied, but that is decidedly different from addressing fundamental sources of instability and injustice. The hardest work in the 1990s surely lies in the realm of politics and diplomacy.

In addition, a substantial group of church leaders expressed shock and frustration over the ordering of priorities. How, they asked, is it possible to mobilize so rapidly, demonstrate such resolve, and spare no expense to face down aggression abroad while major domestic problems—poverty, unemployment, homelessness, inadequate health care, drugs, crime, education—are being largely ignored or treated superficially? When will the U.S. government show such resolve for getting the domestic house in order? In short, some felt that President Bush's unequivocal stance against injustice and oppression was being applied far too selectively.

Roman Catholic and some Protestant leaders focused primarily on the elements of the just war theory. They argued the traditional position that war can be just so long as certain condi-

21

tions are met. In mid-November 1990, the U.S. Conference of Catholic Bishops released a statement including the following questions:

Is the war engaged for a just cause?

Is it authorized by the competent authorities?

Is it undertaken with the right intention, that is, are the stated reasons the actual reasons?

Is war the last resort—have all peaceful alternatives been pursued?

Is the probability of military success sufficient to justify the human costs?

Are the costs of war proportional to the objectives to be achieved?

The Catholic bishops raised serious doubts about several of these questions. The Bush administration had offered various justifications for rapid preparation for war: Hussein's brutal aggression, oil, jobs, economic stability, the integrity of Kuwait, Iraq's nuclear and chemical weapons threat to its neighbors, and the opportunity to begin a new world order. Each issue had arguable merit, but the confusing, sometimes shifting signals from Washington fueled the debate about satisfying the necessary conditions for a just war.

Many doubted that the issue of proportionality could be satisfied. How many Iraqi, Kuwaiti, and Allied coalition lives would be lost? The doubts about proportionality turned out to be well-founded. While the actual totals on the Allied side were far lower than the most optimistic Pentagon estimates, the death figures were high: more than 150,000 Iraqis and several thousand Kuwaitis. The human face of war was rarely visible during the conflict. The horror came more sharply, if briefly, into view some six months later when Pentagon spokesman Pete Wilson confirmed that many Iraqi soldiers were deliberately buried alive during the ground offensive. He did not dispute published estimates of 8,000 Iraqis buried alive. Rather, he noted that there was no way to get an accurate count. Wilson, agreeing that this image was horrible, stated, "There is no nice way to kill people."

The longer term casualties—including Iraqi refugees and tens of thousands of foreign nationals who were forced to flee the area—may never be measurable with any degree of certainty. Some of these casualties, of course, resulted from Iraqi actions quite apart from the Allied military response.

The question of right intention was also seriously debated. The ostensible reasons for the mobilization and war centered on the naked aggression of Iraq and the obvious oppression visited upon the people of Kuwait. Still, many wondered aloud about the unstated importance of other economic and military concerns. Questions about the stated reasons as opposed to the actual reasons resurfaced following the war when the coalition forces chose not to respond with military force to the desperate pleas for assistance from those Iraqis being crushed by Saddam Hussein's military. Hussein's tyranny and oppression were the motivating factors in Kuwait; the tragedy befalling Iraqi civilians, on the other hand, was somehow different; it was, according to Bush Administration officials, an "internal" matter for the people of Iraq.

Others objected strongly to the rush to war as the apparent first, rather than last resort. Had all the options been exhausted? Clearly, many Americans did not believe so. In addition to church leaders, many in Congress, several former Defense Secretaries, heads of the Joint Chiefs of Staff, and leaders of the military branches offered Congressional testimony on this point in the fall of 1990. Moreover, an interesting array of conservative writers and leaders—from Patrick Buchanan to H. Ross Perot—strongly opposed the sequence of events that placed the military option at the head of the list.

After the fact, it is all too easy to forget the ambiguous dynamics in the fall of 1990. Those in the churches who argued on the basis of just war criteria found strong support in Congress. The debates leading up to the Congressional votes authorizing President Bush to use "whatever means were necessary" turned largely on the questions articulated above. Whatever one's position, the serious, often poignant debate was a dramatic illustration

23

of democracy at work. When the two definitive resolutions were addressed on January 12, 1991, 46 U.S. Senators voted in favor of giving sanctions more time, while 53 voted against; 47 voted against the authorization to use force, 52 were in favor.

The various objections and reservations noted above were evident in three public statements issued by Protestant and Orthodox church leaders in the 32 communions comprising the National Council of Churches (NCC). But these church leaders went further. Informed by the broader concerns of the ecumenical movement worldwide, they endeavored to transcend narrowly defined national perspectives and give voice to others in the larger body of Christ, most notably those in the Middle Eastern Christian community. Although indigenous Arabic-speaking Christians in the Middle East number more than 12 million—a community four times the size of the Jewish population in Israel—most Americans seem unaware of their existence. It is sadly ironic that the oldest Christian communities, which still inhabit the very lands where the church was born, are so invisible in the West.

In early November, 1990, the NCC's General Board adopted a resolution strongly opposing the build-up toward war. Its sharp criticism of the American-led response to the crisis reflected deep-seated fears present among most Middle Eastern Christians: that widespread human suffering and long-term economic dislocation would flow from war; that extremist positions would be strengthened and solidified; and that relations between the Christian minority and Muslim majority, already strained in several countries, could be damaged further by the rhetoric and actions of political leaders justifying their behavior by appealing to their respective religious traditions.

To understand better the concerns of Middle Eastern Christians, 18 U.S. church leaders (including the official heads of ten communions, e.g., American Baptist, Episcopal, Lutheran, Presbyterian, Reformed, United Church of Christ, United Methodist, etc.) traveled to the Middle East in mid-December. They met with representatives of the Middle East Council of Churches (MECC), an ecumenical body that includes virtually all Christians—Orthodox, Catholic, and Protestant. The group then dispersed for visits to Baghdad, Beirut, and Jerusalem. Upon returning to the U.S., these leaders issued a "Message to the American people," entitled "War Is Not the Answer." The message spoke directly to the impending war and its potential consequences, but also to the deep, longstanding conflicts that threaten the entire region.

> One clear message emerged from our many conversations in these holy lands: "War would be a disaster for us all." We were told time and again, "Please go home and tell the American people that a way to peace can and must be found." We have concluded that in the Middle East today it is no longer only a question of right and wrong; it is also a matter of life and death.[2]

Upon his return from this sojourn to Cyprus, Jordan, and Iraq, the Presiding Bishop of the Episcopal Church, Edmond Browning, met privately for 40 minutes with President Bush and Secretary of State James A. Baker III. Bishop Browning, a seasoned leader with a longstanding concern for Middle East issues, conveyed his impressions of the fears and frustrations of many with whom he met. He urged the President not to pursue the war option. They clearly did not view the issues in the same way. The President admitted that he "hated to have his bishop in opposition." At the conclusion of their meeting, Bishop Browning assured President Bush that he would continue to pray for him every day.

Bishop Browning and many prominent ecumenical leaders also continued to speak out in opposition to the military option, even after the war began in mid-January. In the words of United Methodist Bishop Melvin G. Talbert, "The most patriotic thing religious leaders in our country can do is stop the war." The strongest collective statement came on February 13, 1991, when more than 100 church leaders from virtually every Protestant, Catholic, and Orthodox communion issued "A Call to the Churches." While most of the country seemed caught up in a patriotic fervor fed by military dominance, these religious leaders offered an alternative witness. Once again and with a renewed sense of urgency, these Christians called the churches to responsible domestic pastoral ministry even as they articulated the heart-

---

2. "War is Not the Answer: A Message to the American People," (Dec. 22, 1990). The statement was released through the media. For the full text, see *Sojourners* magazine (Feb.-Mar., 1991), p. 5.

felt concerns of Middle Eastern Christians. A brief excerpt from
the two-page document illustrates the point:

> Let our churches embrace the bereaved, maimed and homeless of
> the Middle East through a generous response to the ministry of
> compassion. . . . Let our churches reach out in a spirit of dialogue
> and seek ways to bring Muslims, Christians and Jews together to
> address our fears, concerns and hopes for peace.

The desire to serve others with a cup of cool water, food,
medical care, and safe housing is not only a biblical imperative, it
is the operative manifestation of Christian presence and witness
in the predominantly Muslim Middle East. Over and above national or even religious group interests, people of faith must put
priority on the human interest. These concerns, unnoticed or
dismissed by most Americans during the war, moved to center
stage in the aftermath of the war. The "Call" seemed like a voice
crying in the wilderness in February; it appeared prophetic by
April when the need for such ministry became clear to all.

Further, the "Call" reflected the Middle Eastern Christians'
view that the only viable future is a shared future. The children
of Abraham—Jews, Christians, and Muslims—must find more constructive ways to relate to one another in coming years. The crisis
and war in the Gulf represent a critical point in this process. The
high visibility of these traumatic events has created an unprecedented opportunity to understand better the crosscurrents affect-
ing the Middle East and our future role and responsibilities as
concerned people of faith. We look back in order that we can see
how best to move forward into an uncertain future. The challenge
for the children of Abraham goes beyond simple tolerance; mutual understanding and cooperation are required if we are to
continue to share an increasingly fragile and interdependent
planet.

The war in the Gulf and its aftermath have made clear how
little most Western Christians know about Islam and the forces at
work within that tradition. We begin, therefore, with a look at
Islam in chapter 1. Developing a clearer picture of the dominant
religious tradition and demystifying the image of Islam in the Gulf
war is crucial; it provides an invaluable backdrop against which it

is easier to identify and understand the confusing political dynamics operative in the modern Middle East.

Chapter 2 explores major features of the political landscape in this fascinating region. Here we seek to assess the major sources of regional instability that surfaced visibly during the crisis. Understanding these root causes and convoluted political dynamics is vital if we hope to move forward on the difficult road toward peace.

Finally, in chapter 3, we turn to the converging issues of oil, arms sales and transfers, and economic interdependence. The challenges posed are many as these global issues are played out in microcosm within the Middle Eastern nation-states.

Each chapter seeks to build upon the experiences and insights discernible in the Gulf war in an effort to broaden awareness of regional dynamics and identify constructive ways to move forward. The task requires sorting through the differences between image and reality.

Religion, politics, and oil make for a volatile mix. The explosive, highly charged nature of the interrelated issues underscores the necessity of developing a more coherent framework of understanding. Our approach is introductory, not exhaustive. Selected resources for additional, more in-depth study are included in an annotated bibliography at the end of the book.

The crisis in the Gulf has provided a window through which we can view and seek to understand the challenges and opportunities present in the lands still cherished by the descendants of Abraham. Responsible ministry through the churches and responsible citizenship in the world's most powerful country require that we seize the moment. There are no easy answers or simple solutions. But, as people of faith, with God's help, we can pursue a ministry of reconciliation, peacemaking, and compassionate service in the name of Jesus, the pioneer and perfecter of our faith.

CHAPTER 1

Religion

We in Iraq will be the faithful and obedient servants of God, struggling for his sake to raise the banner of truth and justice, the banner of "God is greater!" . . . It remains for us to tell all the faithful strugglers: you have a duty to carry out holy war and struggle in order to target the assembly of evil, treason and corruption everywhere. (Saddam Hussein, speaking on Radio Baghdad, January 20, 1991)

It is a just war. . . . Our cause could not be more noble . . . entrusted with the holy gift of freedom, and allowed to prosper in its great light, we have a responsibility to serve as a beacon to the world. . . . God bless the United States of America. (George Bush, addressing the National Religious Broadcasters Convention, January 31, 1991)

And what does the Lord require of you but to do justice, and to love kindness, and to walk humbly with your God? (Micah 6:8, NRSV)

The war in the Gulf was not religiously based. The sources of conflict were primarily political and economic. Even so, "religion" figured prominently in the numerous events framing and influencing the unfolding drama. For most Americans, the barrage of Islamic images added confusing elements to an already complicated picture.

Saddam Hussein's repeated calls for "holy war" and his use of religious rhetoric served to reinforce a longstanding Western stereotype of Islam as somehow inherently fanatic, violent, and menacing. At the same time, more positive pictures depicted pious Saudi, Kuwaiti, and Egyptian Muslims participating bravely in the front lines of the U.S.-led Allied coalition. Other striking images were also juxtaposed. Some journalists reported on the repressive and restrictive conditions experienced by Saudi women, for instance; other stories featured surprising portrayals of "moderate" Iranian leaders offering to facilitate a peace process. Among the complement of photographs featured in various newspapers, readers saw memorable images of Saudis at prayer wearing gas masks, an American Muslim member of the Marine Corps praying alone in the desert, and an F-16 fighter jet flying low over a mosque in Turkey en route to a target in northern Iraq.

The massive media coverage failed to produce a more coherent understanding of Islam in the West. It did, however, underscore the central role of this religious community on the world stage. Muslims today number more than one billion adherents. Now, perhaps more than ever, it is imperative that we in the predominantly Christian West endeavor to understand more accurately some fundamental tenets of Islam, the world's second largest religious tradition. Such understanding is the point of departure for the effort to clarify the role of Islam in the Gulf war as well as in a variety of settings throughout the world.

Toward Understanding Islam and the Muslims

The central message of Islam is lodged in the simple confession of faith: "There is no god but God, and Muhammad is the messenger of God." Islam is a radical monotheism. Muslims affirm one true God as Creator and Sustainer of the universe whose will has been manifest to humankind through prophetic revelation. They believe that this revelation is now contained in the Qur'an, which they consider to be the literal, perfect, and complete word of God, and that the proper human response to this revelation is obedience both in worship of God and in all aspects of life.

A brief Arabic lesson helps to demystify the fundamental meaning of key terms and make clear the basic orientation of Muslims. Like Hebrew, Arabic is built on a consonantal root system. Most words are derived from three consonants which convey a basic notion. The letters *k-t-b*, for instance, relate to the idea of writing. When different vowels, prefixes, or suffixes are added, words are formed. Thus *kataba* means "he wrote"; a *kitab* is a "book"; a *maktab* is an "office" (a place where writing occurs); a *maktabah* is a "library"; and so forth.

The root meanings of *s-l-m* have to do with submission to the will of God and peace. Three familiar words derive from this root: *salam*, *Islam* and *Muslim*. "Salam" means "peace, well-being"; it originates from the same root as the more familiar Hebrew word *shalom*. (The "s" and "sh" are distinctive letters in Arabic and Hebrew; they are often transposed in usage in these two Semitic languages.) Islam literally means "submission to the will of God"; it is "the religion of peace." Those who submit themselves in obedience to God are Muslims; they are, by definition, people "at peace" in creation.

Muslims worship the same God as Christians and Jews. Many non-Arabic speakers, confused by the name Allah, have not made this connection. Allah is simply the Arabic term for God. The 10 to 12 million indigenous Arabic-speaking Christians in the Middle East today pray to Allah, just as the French pray to Dieu and Germans to Gott. For Muslims there is no ambiguity here: the one, true God is the God of Abraham, Moses, Jesus, Muhammad, and everyone else in creation.

As with Christianity, foundational doctrines and devotional practices in Islam can be described in a relatively straightforward manner. The vitality of the religious tradition as embraced and lived out by faithful adherents is a far more subtle and complex matter. Christians, for example, believe that Jesus, the incarnation of God, died for the sins of the world and was resurrected miraculously by God. These affirmations provide little indication, however, of how people of faith have, in different times and places, appropriated the implications of Jesus' life, death, and resurrection. The same is true for Islam. Descriptive accounts of basic teachings are helpful, but they fail to convey the texture and diversity found within the history of this extensive religious tradition.

In 610, at the age of 40, Muhammad had a profound and disturbing experience which he understood as a revelation from God. During one of his periodic sojourns for meditation and reflection at Mt. Hira, near Mecca, he saw a radiant figure on the horizon coming toward him. The figure, perceived to be the angel Gabriel, drew near and pronounced the first of the messages Muhammad was instructed to communicate. The account of Muhammad's reaction to this experience after his return to Mecca is reminiscent of many of the Hebrew prophets. He was terribly shaken by the episode; he doubted both his sanity and his worthiness to be God's prophetic messenger. Encouraged by his wife and a few close friends, he came to accept this responsibility.

Throughout the 23 years following this first encounter, Muhammad continued to receive messages. He would recite these, and others would both memorize and write down the revelations. The totality of these utterances comprise the Qur'an. The magnificence of the poetic text, uttered by a man known to be unlettered, has always been interpreted by Muslims as proof of the miraculous process of revelation. Listening to qur'anic recitation leaves little doubt about the lyrical quality and majesty of the text–even if the hearer does not know Arabic, but all the more if she or he does.

Roughly the length of the New Testament, the Qur'an is divided into 114 chapters, called *surahs*. The number of verses, each called an *ayah*, in the chapters varies greatly. With the notable exception of the first *surah*, the Qur'an is arranged generally according to the length of the chapter with the longest ones first. This arrangement is roughly in reverse chronological order in which the messages were proclaimed. Thus, the shortest chapters, found toward the end of the Qur'an, were among the first Meccan *surahs*; the longer, Medinan chapters are found in the front of the collection. For the person new to the text, this arrangement sometimes creates confusion. Rather than simply picking up the text and beginning to read, the student wishing to study the Qur'an is well-advised to seek assistance.

The glorious majesty of God, reflected in the attributes associated with the 99 names of God (e.g., All-Knowing, All-Powerful,

All-Compassionate), is central throughout the Qur'an. While God is the transcendent Lord of all creation, God is also intimately connected with human beings. The immanence of God is portrayed as being closer to humans than their jugular vein (Qur'an 50:16).

Heaven and hell, human responsibility and the certainty of judgement on the Last Day are all vividly proclaimed. While the Qur'an does not present a systematic exposition, it does include a body of doctrine and practical obligations. Social and ethical parameters are set in areas such as: marriage and divorce; inheritance; commercial dealings; responsibility toward children; the care of widows, orphans, and others among the less fortunate in society; and such criminal behavior as theft, murder, and adultery.

Muslims believe that Muhammad was the last in a long succession of prophetic messengers sent to humankind. Many of the prophets named in the Qur'an are also major figures in the Bible. These include Noah, Abraham, Moses, David, John the Baptist, and Jesus. Most Christians are surprised to discover the importance Muslims attach to Jesus. Mentioned by name in 93 different verses, Jesus is venerated as one of the greatest prophets. He is unique by virtue of the miraculous virgin birth as well as his distinctive names. Jesus is called a "word" from God, the "messiah," and "a spirit from God." In the final analysis, however, Muslims are clear: Jesus, like all the prophets, was human.

The error of his followers, according to the Qur'an, is that they claim things about Jesus–namely, that he was God's son, that he was divine, that he was resurrected by God and is now part of the Trinity–that Jesus never claimed for himself. These are dangerous teachings in the Islamic understanding because they challenge the absolute oneness and unity of God. Accordingly, the Qur'an includes stern words of warning for Christians and others who associate anything so immediately with God.

Grave warnings against doctrinal error notwithstanding, the Qur'an makes clear that the religious communities should exist in complete freedom. A famous qur'anic declaration asserts, "There shall be no compulsion in religious matters" (Qur'an 2:256). The closeness and saving value of the religions practiced by the "people of the book" is stated explicitly:

> Behold! Those who have faith, and those who are Jews, Christians and Sabaeans–those who trust in God and the Last Day, and do what is righteous, they shall have their reward; no fear shall come upon them, neither shall they grieve. (Qur'an 2:62 and 5:69)

As with all human history and experience, there exists a gap between the principles and ideals in the religious tradition–as articulated by a founder, its sacred text(s) or the wisdom of tradition–and the practice of the adherents through the years. Accordingly, Islamic history includes numerous instances where this kind of openness is obscured by hostility and intolerance.

In addition to conveying the content of the revelation, Muhammad also proffered advice and made clear his perspectives on a wide range of subjects. The Qur'an points people of faith to the exemplary life and behavior of Muhammad as a source for guidance in daily life: "Truly in the messenger of God you have a beautiful model" (Qur'an 33:21). From the outset, faithful Muslims endeavored to record accurately the traditions (*hadith*) of their prophet. Elaborate methods were developed to preserve the authentic words and deeds of Muhammad. Collectively, the sayings and actions of Muhammad are called the *sunnah* (the "path" or "practice"). While Muslims have always been careful to clarify that Muhammad was a man and in no way to be deified, his particular role has led, in fact, to special veneration at the popular level.

The life of faith begins with the confession, "There is no god but God, and Muhammad is the Prophet of God," called the *shahadah*. Joyful gratitude and obedience to the Creator are manifest in worship and adherence to the requirements established in the Qur'an and other sources of authority. The obligatory core components are delineated in five devotional-ritual duties called the "pillars of Islam." The first pillar is the *shahadah*.

Prescribed prayer, *salat*, is the second and most conspicuous manifestation of faith. Five times daily, Muslims are called to prayer from the tall *minarets* in the mosques. Any non-Muslim visiting in a predominantly Muslim country is familiar with the call to prayer echoing throughout the city; most have had the experience of being jolted awake prior to dawn when the first prayer takes place. This common experience fosters a new level

34

of appreciation for the commitment required for such devotional piety. The actual prayer ritual combines several cycles of prayer (primarily recitation of qur'anic passages committed to memory) with different body postures. The worshipers stand in rows of straight lines oriented toward the *Ka'bah*, the central sacred site in Mecca. The symbolic unity of Muslims in prayer reflects the conviction that all people stand equally before God.

The third pillar of Islam is almsgiving or religious contribution (*zakat*). Each year, Muslims are expected to give 2.5% of their overall wealth for the poor and less fortunate. *Zakat* is a religious duty which reflects the conviction that one's resources derive from God. As an institutional form of stewardship, *zakat* is an effective way to support the needs of the poor within the community and thereby strengthen the whole.

Each year, Muslims are required to fast (*sawm*) during the daylight hours of the month of Ramadan. The fast is supposed to be a time for self-discipline and serious reflection. Among its benefits, Muslims cite the sense of unity experienced in fasting. Those things that normally divide people–status, class, wealth, race–are removed in the common experience. Moreover, the deprivation increases awareness of the plight of those less fortunate, those who do not enjoy the basic necessities. The fast of Ramadan, which began in mid-March, received unusual attention in 1991 because many feared the unifying religious practice might complicate the potentially fragile alliances in the Gulf war.

The final pillar is the pilgrimage (*hajj*) to Mecca. At some point in life, Muslims are expected to take part in the elaborate pilgrimage during the time set apart for the annual ritual. All believers long to take part in the pilgrimage; many literally save money for a lifetime in order to make the trip to Mecca. Each year, more than two million adherents arrive by land, sea, and air to take part in the various rituals spanning several days. Pilgrims don a simple white garment made of two white seamless pieces of cloth, an act which once again symbolizes the equality of all people before God. The King of Saudi Arabia wears the same garment and worships alongside a person from the lowest strata of Indian society. The days of pilgrimage unite Muslims from all over the world even as the rituals link them with special events in their history.

Woven through these devotional-ritual practices are threads uniting Muslims as equal members of the community of faith. Individual responsibility is continuously linked with the well-being of the whole. This community is known as the *ummah*. The *ummah* represented a new and radical departure from the social organization of the Arabian clans. The corporate identity within the *ummah* has been a powerful and distinctive characteristic uniting Muslims over the centuries.

This does not mean, however, that all has been harmonious within the "house of Islam." On the contrary, Islamic history is filled with the same types of schism, power struggles, and political and military conflicts as one finds in all of human history. The reality on the ground does not always match the stated ideal. Ask several Muslim women from different countries about equality in Islam and you will find no consensus. As one Saudi woman put it during the Gulf war, "Some people are more equal than others!" In fact, a close look at Islamic history reveals patterns that are common in other communities: a rich tradition, inspiring people to their highest good and, at the same time, one replete with fourteen centuries of human foibles.

One of the first major internal controversies surfaced at the time of Muhammad's death. The Muslims were not in agreement concerning the temporal leadership of the community. Some argued that Muhammad had designated Ali, who was both his cousin and son-in-law, as his successor. The group was known as the *shi'ah* (the "party" or "faction" supporting Ali; Latinized as Shi'ites). They did not prevail. The majority of Muhammad's closest companions agreed instead on Abu Bakr as the proper successor or *khalifa* (Caliph). Abu Bakr led the community from 632 to 634, followed by Umar (634–44) and Uthman (644–56). Finally, after nearly a quarter-century, the internal debate about leadership appeared to be resolved when Ali was selected as the fourth *khalifa* in 656. He ruled for five tumultuous years until his assassination in 661.

With Ali's death, the community was even more deeply divided. The Shi'ites argued for continuing leadership in the family of the prophet through his grandsons (Ali's sons). The larger majority, those who came to be known as the *Sunnis* (the "orthodox"), rejected this argument. These were critical, formative years for the nascent community. Numerous logistical problems associated with the rapid success and expansion of Islam combined with festering internal disagreements. The result was open conflict. In 680, the strong military forces of the Sunni *khalifa* clashed with a small group of Shi'ites led by Husayn, the grandson of Muhammad. The Shi'ites were annihilated at Karbala, a city in the southern portion of present-day Iraq. From that time forward, Shi'ites have commemorated the martyrdom of the faithful and incorporated redemptive suffering into their theological understandings.

What began as a question of succession developed over the centuries into substantial differences in theology and worldview between Sunnis and Shi'ites. Within each of the two large branches, various schools developed around theological, philosophical, and legal interpretations. The study of the intellectual developments within Islam reveals how rich and diverse are the components that comprise the mosaic. Overall, the Sunnis account for approximately 80-85% and the Shi'ites 15-20% of the total Muslim population today. Apart from a few instances, Shi'ite leaders have not controlled temporal power. The rise to power of Shi'ite religious leaders through the 1979 revolution in Iran, a country whose populace is over 90% Shi'ite, is one of the exceptions.

The second largest concentration of Shi'ites today is found in Iraq. This community, primarily lodged in the southern part of the country, accounts for more than 60% of the population. They were particularly visible in the Gulf war because of their concentration in the primary war zone. In addition, the Iraqi Shi'ites, encouraged by neighboring Iran, and the Kurdish people in the northern part of Iraq, were the primary groups rising up in rebellion against Saddam Hussein. While these uprisings were suppressed brutally by government forces, the Shi'ite majority remains a major factor in Iraq's political and religious landscape.

A smaller, but nonetheless formidable Shi'ite population resides in Lebanon. Some within this community have been highly visible in the decade since the 1982 Israeli invasion of Lebanon. The Shi'ites were the most persistent force combating the Israeli occupation in the southern third of their country. Several of the most extremist Shi'ite groups have been notorious for their role in the seizing and holding of Western men as hostages.

Popular perceptions in the West often connect Shi'ite Islam with conservative and extremist movements. While individuals and some groups within the minority Shi'ites have been highly visible, they are by no means alone. Numerous Sunni-based groups and movements throughout the world are both susbstantial and active forces for political change. Some work within political structures; some operate underground for fear of persecution from existing governments.

Islam has always been a major force in the political realm. From modest origins in seventh-century Arabia, Muslims burst on the scene and spread rapidly northward into the Fertile Crescent, west across North Africa and east through the ancient lands of the Tigris and Euphrates valleys into central Asia. Within a century of Muhammad's death, the domain of Islam stretched from southern Spain to the northwest portion of India.

The unparalleled success in this phenomenal growth was due in part to the zealous faith and military prowess of the first generations of Arab Muslims as well as the decadent state of the Mediterranean world. After this initial outward thrust, Islam continued to spread through the persuasive power of its message, often carried by merchants, and its vibrant, thriving civilization. The Western image of Islam as inherently backward, anti-intellectual and unsophisticated quickly disappears in the face of even a cursory survey of Islamic history. The error of the image is particularly ironic in view of the major contributions and influences that helped shape Western civilization as we know it today. Indigenous Arab Christians and Christian converts to Islam were also very much a part of this process, but the dominant impetus came from within Islam itself.

A sampling of English words originating with Muslim cultures provides a clue to primary areas of influence: admiral, adobe, alchemy, alcohol, alcove, alfalfa, algebra, amulet, arsenal, artichoke, assassin, average, balcony, banana, cable, candy, checkmate, coffee, cotton, divan, elixir, frieze, gala, giraffe, guitar, jasmine, lemon, lute, magazine, mask, mat, monsoon, musk, nadir, orange, rice, safari, sapphire, sofa, sugar, syrup, tariff, troubadour, zenith, zero.

When Europe was languishing in the "Dark Ages," Islamic civilization was thriving from Spain, across North Africa, through the Fertile Crescent and Mesopotamia, and into India. Most people are surprised to discover the substantial contributions of Muslims in science, engineering, navigation, mathematics, chemistry, medicine, astronomy, philosophy, architecture, horticulture, and calligraphy. Muslims are very proud of their history and civilization.

Following centuries of unprecedented growth and development, the extensive Islamic empire entered a long period of uneven decline after the fall of Baghdad to the Mongol invaders in 1258. Various political and military developments altered the map in Asia and the Mediterranean region. Some portions of the Islamic world continued to flourish while other areas were subjugated to external rule. From the 16th to the 20th centuries, most of the lands with a Muslim majority were under the control of outside political powers. This reality provides the backdrop that helps to interpret contemporary upheavals and resurgence movements among Muslims today.

The Islamic revival surged into popular consciousness in the West with the 1979 Iranian revolution. In fact, various elements of the reform and renewal movement had been developing during the past two centuries. John Esposito, a well-known student of contemporary Islam, summarized current developments in an article on "Islamic Revivalism":

> Islamic revivalism in its broadest sense refers to a renewal of Islam in Muslim personal and public life. Its manifestations include an increase in religious observances (mosque attendance, Ramadan fast, wearing traditional Islamic dress); a revitalization of sufi (mystical) orders; proliferation of religious publications and media programming; calls for the implementation of Islamic law; creation of Islamic banks; and the growth of Islamic organizations and activist movements.

Growing out of this context, Islamic revivalism has led to the reassertion of Islam in politics. Incumbent governments appeal to Islam for political legitimacy and popular support for policies and programs. Opposition movements use the language and symbols of Islam to criticize established governments, and to advocate actions ranging from socio-political reform to violent revolutionary action.

The forms that Islamic revivalism take vary almost infinitely from one country to another, but there are certain themes: a sense that existing political, economic, and social systems have failed; a disenchantment with and even rejection of the West; a quest for identity and greater authenticity; and the conviction that Islam provides a self-sufficient ideology for state and society, a valid alternative to secular nationalism, socialism, and capitalism.[1]

Esposito's emphasis on the diversity found in different countries should be underscored. Any effort to understand the dynamics related to upheaval or the demand for change must take seriously the particular context. Sweeping generalizations devoid of contextual analysis inevitably lead to erroneous conclusions. Although Great Britain, Sweden, France and Italy are all Western European countries with predominantly Christian populations, no serious person wanting to understand developments in these countries would offer casual generalizations and assume they would fit in all four contexts. Similarly, Lebanon, Algeria, Egypt, and Iraq represent four very distinct settings, each requiring analysis on its own terms.

Esposito also accurately identifies common themes and concerns discernible among many Muslim groups. These themes—centering on disenchantment with the West and the conviction that Islam can provide a comprehensive framework for state and society—are evident throughout the Muslim world; and, they are increasingly powerful factors in the political sphere. The importance of these widely held views is visible in the rhetoric employed by most individual Muslim leaders and groups who seek popular support.

In the weeks following his invasion of Kuwait, Saddam Hussein overtly aligned himself with these deep-seated concerns and frustrations. He appealed to popular sentiment through an array

1. John L. Esposito, "Islamic Revivalism," The Muslim World Today, Occasional Paper No. 3 (Washington, DC: American Institute for Islamic Affairs, 1985), p. 1.

of political and religious pronouncements. While his efforts enjoyed only partial success, they underscored the potency of Islam as a factor in contemporary politics.

The Appeal to Popular Religious Sentiment

Religion has always been a powerful force in society. Political leaders know this well and, not surprisingly, often consciously appeal to popular religious sentiment in an effort to bolster support for their policies. Both Saddam Hussein and George Bush did this in the context of the Gulf crisis. For many in the West, the ploy by Saddam Hussein was transparent; for many others, Hussein's rhetoric simply reinforced longstanding images and stereotypes about Islam. George Bush, on the other hand, appealed to religious sentiment in a more subtle, but still quite deliberate manner. A brief look at the behavior of both leaders illuminates patterns that are now and will continue to be operative in the political arena.

Saddam Hussein is not a religious leader. He is a brutal, secular leader who "got religion" in August of 1990–soon after his ill-fated invasion of neighboring Kuwait. His newfound zeal for Islam was little more than a blatant and cynical attempt to deflect attention from his invasion of Kuwait and rally support for political policies he promised to champion.

Hussein's religious rhetoric during the war featured several components: repeated calls for a *jihad* (usually translated "holy war"), the sewing of the familiar Arabic words such as "God is Greater" (*Allahu akbar!*) on the Iraqi flag, continual references to the illegitimacy of the Saudi government for inviting masses of "infidels" to the Arabian peninsula and thereby somehow desecrating the sacred lands of Islam (a reference to Mecca and Medina, places where non-Muslims are prohibited), and a pledge to liberate Jerusalem (the third most sacred site in Islam).

In an effort to demonstrate the support of the religious establishment, Saddam convened several hundred religious leaders in early January 1991. The unofficial gathering included most

Iraqi Muslim leaders as well as representatives from a variety of Muslim groups and movements outside Iraq. After two days of predictable speeches, those assembled dutifully provided the imprimatur Saddam desired. While many Muslims elsewhere were distressed by this event, people outside Iraq could only watch as Saddam Hussein evoked the type of uncritical support that had become a trademark of his political leadership. Various motives prompted the participants living outside Iraq. Participation for Iraqi Muslims, on the other hand, was obligatory: there was no room for dissent, at least for those who wished to see the sun shine the next morning.

A truer picture of a major segment of Iraqi Muslim sentiment was visible in the immediate aftermath of the Gulf war. Within days of the formal cease-fire, Shi'ites in southern Iraq led the insurgent forces seeking to topple Saddam's regime. They seized control of several major cities. Religious leaders, together with their Shi'ite compatriots in neighboring Iran, moved into the forefront of news. U.S. reaction was mixed. On one hand, there was deep animosity toward Saddam Hussein, the leader President Bush described as a new incarnation of Hitler. On the other hand, a successful revolt in southern Iraq might produce another Iran. Consider the irony: a successful revolt against Saddam Hussein, a desirable development, would facilitate the spreading of Iran's Islamic revolution–precisely the concern that prompted the U.S. to provide substantial support for Saddam Hussein's Iraq throughout the 1980s!

Hussein's appeal to religious sentiment should be understood in context. For over eight years during Iraq's bloody war with Iran, the Iranian leadership employed Islamic language and imagery in opposition to Iraq's secular regime. Having observed first hand the power of its popular appeal, Saddam Hussein clearly determined to adopt a new strategy. His efforts did appeal to some Muslims at a popular level. However, most were not taken in by the ploy. A closer look at the notion of *jihad* helps to clarify the point.

The Western media focused considerable attention on Hussein's call for "holy war"; they paid far less attention to the pronouncements of legitimate Muslim authorities elsewhere,

42

most of whom rejected Saddam Hussein. In fact, leading Muslims in Saudi Arabia declared a "holy war" against Iraq in January, 1991.

Few Muslims embraced the Iraqi leader's call for *jihad*. First, he had no religious authority for such a declaration. Second, most Muslims know well the primary and deeper meaning of the Arabic term *jihad*. Like the New Testament, the Qur'an enjoins the faithful to maintain a continual struggle against the frailties and selfish desires that hinder human beings from identifying and following the will of God. In Islam, this great, ongoing struggle for moral perfection is known as *jihad* ("strenuous effort," "striving in the way of God"). Historically, the meaning of *jihad* as outward struggle–particularly in the context of military confrontation–has always been secondary. In recent years, however, numerous religious and political zealots have emphasized this secondary meaning in the midst of political machinations.

Despite this, it is also important to understand that there was considerable popular support for Saddam Hussein in religious circles. Why? The answer lies in the political developments in the region. Many contemporary Muslims believe that political changes are both possible and necessary. And they argue fervently that Islam can provide the political, religious and economic frameworks for their societies. A political leader, even one as unsavory as Hussein, who is perceived–rightly or wrongly–as standing up to the forces that are believed to block such changes finds a great deal of support among some frustrated Muslims.

Popular religious sentiment also figured into the war from the U.S. side. From the beginning, President Bush employed religious language to rally public support for his policy decisions. On August 8, 1990, the President addressed the nation in order to announce the decision to deploy a major U.S. military presence. The televised speech concluded with these words:

> Standing up for our principles will not come easy. It may take time and possibly cost a great deal. But, we are asking no more of anyone than of the brave young men and women in our armed forces. And, I ask that in churches around this country prayers be said for those who are committed to protect American interests.
>
> Standing up for our principles is an American tradition. As it

has so many times before, it will take tremendous effort. But, most of all, it will take unity of purpose. As I have witnessed throughout my life–in both war and peace–America has never waivered when her purpose was driven by principle. And, in this August day–at home and abroad–I know she will do no less. Thank you and God bless the United States of America.

President Bush's appeal to popular Christian sentiment was less blatant than Saddam Hussein's appeal to Islam. Even so, it was obvious: virtually every speech ended with the words "God bless the United States of America"; several Sundays were designated as national days of prayer, marked by the ringing of church bells; the Rev. Billy Graham was Mr. Bush's highly visible overnight guest on January 15, 1991.

Perhaps the most striking religious feature was the moral basis upon which the U.S. actions were ostensibly based. President Bush and other Administration officials underscored time and again the morality of the war as the means to halt aggression and tyranny. In the weeks leading up to war and during the actual combat the President spoke passionately and consistently about good versus evil, right versus wrong, the moral use of force, religious values, and God's blessing on the U.S.A.

With religious rhetoric and imagery present on both sides of the Gulf war, various journalists wrestled with the question, "Whose side is God on?" Perhaps the most poignant response to that query came from Gabriel Habib, the General Secretary of the Middle East Council of Churches. When asked whose side he thought God was on, Habib paused then said, "God is on the side of those who suffer."

Learning from the Gulf Crisis[2]

There are many lessons to be learned from the traumatic events surrounding the Gulf war. High on the list are lessons about Islam. Islamic institutions and Muslims motivated by their

2. The "lessons" identified in this section include and expand upon points first published in Charles Kimball, "Prospects for a Postwar Order: Hard Work Ahead—Aid and Understanding," *The Christian Century* (April 10, 1991), pp. 396-7.

faith are playing an increasingly important role in a variety of countries in transition to new political structures. This phenomenon was illustrated vividly in the disquieting public demonstrations by Muslims in settings as diverse as Morocco, Pakistan, and Indonesia. In many parts of the Muslim world large groups–often hundreds of thousands–massed in public opposition to the U.S.-led build-up to and prosecution of the war.

In order to understand these dynamics, it is critical to recall Esposito's comments concerning the Islamic revival movement. A growing number of Muslims are calling for political reform based somehow on Islam. Any major leader who appears to champion that cause in defiance of geopolitical realities will find considerable support. The strength of the Ayatollah Khomeini's popular appeal in the 1980s, not necessarily his particular theological framework, related to this phenomenon.

Another clarifying factor is contextual analysis. When one begins to look specifically at the countries where the largest public demonstrations occurred, a pattern begins to emerge: deep discontent with domestic politics figured prominently in the protest. In Pakistan, for instance, the driving force for organized protest came from a religious party advocating Islamic law in the country. In late January 1991, one commentator in Bangladesh observed that the upcoming national elections were being sorted out "in the mosques" through public positions on the war in the Gulf.

At a time when Islamic groups and Muslims motivated by their faith are playing a central role in such turbulent political developments it is surprising to realize how little most North Americans know about the world's second largest religious tradition. Regrettably, the ignorance of religious and cultural dynamics extends throughout the U.S. government. If the U.S. hopes to help resolve daunting and persistent conflicts peacefully, this problem must be addressed. The U.S. must find ways to understand more fully and enter respectfully into the particular dynamics of various countries. One step would be to include more area and Islamic specialists in the ranks of the Foreign Service. The current paucity of such specialists stands in stark contrast to the abundance of knowledgeable political, military, and economic advisors staffing U.S. embassies worldwide.

Another lesson from this crisis centers on the positive cooperation across religious lines which took place during the war. Cynical, polarizing rhetoric notwithstanding, the Gulf war was not religiously based. In fact, Christians and Muslims worked, fought, and died together. This experience of cooperation in a common cause must not be lost. Rather, it is crucial to find ways to build upon it in the coming years. The multiple challenges facing the world community–major threats to the ecosystem, the rampaging AIDS epidemic, unspeakable poverty, and the plight of millions of refugees–require the best efforts of all people of goodwill.

In view of the deep bias and prevalent misperceptions about Islam, various institutions in the U.S.–from the churches to the government–should seize the initiative to remedy the situation. Major efforts are needed to stimulate communication, foster understanding, help correct negative stereotypes, and encourage cooperation across religious lines. Long-term cultural exchanges and people-to-people programs will help demystify and put a human face on the "other." The pattern and benefits of the contacts and exchanges between U.S. and Soviet citizens during the 1980s provide an instructive model.

Christians in the West must make concerted efforts to break through the images and stereotypes and come to a more accurate understanding of Islam. At the conclusion of the war, General Norman Schwarzkopf spoke directly to this point. Addressing departing troops on March 8, 1991, the Allied commander offered the following remarks:

> You served in a place I'm sure none of you thought you'd serve. You've been places you never heard of. You've been places you can't even pronounce. But you also better take back with you some free lessons that your family, friends and the world can hear.
>
> You're going to take back the fact that the word "Arab" isn't a bad word. That you do not judge all Arabs by the actions of a few. And I know here that we have close, wonderful, warm and thankful people for us being here and [they] have expressed that thanks in many different ways.
>
> And you are going to take back the fact that "Islam" is not a word to be feared, it is a religion to be respected, just as we respect all religions. That's the American way.

General Schwarzkopf's observations and advice reflect a wisdom born of experience. We would all do well both to ponder the significance of these words and seek peaceful ways to live out the implications.

A good place to begin building bridges of understanding is within the domestic realm. Muslims now constitute a sizable religious community in the U.S. They are increasing rapidly as second, third, and fourth generation families come on to the scene, as well as through immigration and conversion. The U.S. government has an important role to play in making audible the concerns, hopes, and fears of American Muslims. One important step would be to provide political access for this community. Protestant, Catholic, and Orthodox Christians, as well as American Jews, have long had staff contact persons in the President's Office of Public Liaison. Access and visibility for American Muslims is long overdue.

Concerned Christians and churches have many opportunities to work constructively in the interfaith arena. Focused educational programs–either through adult study groups or church-wide programs or both–provide an excellent place to begin improving understanding of Islam and relations with Muslims. Most of the larger denominational bodies have staff and resources to assist in this effort. Many local, statewide, and national ecumenical organizations provide structures and offer appropriate programs. In addition to educational initiatives, programs for stuctured dialogue with Muslims and cooperative efforts on shared concerns in local communities can be highly productive.

In the wake of the Gulf war we can see more clearly than ever the importance of Christian-Muslim relations. Together, these religious communities comprise approximately half of the world's population. The ways in which adherents in these two communities relate to one another in the final decade of the twentieth century will have profound consequences for both communities— and for the the world.

CHAPTER 2

Politics

From Madrid, let us light the candle of peace, and let the olive branch blossom. Let us celebrate the rituals of justice and rejoice in the hymns of truth, for the awe of the moment is a promise to the future, which we all must redeem. (Dr. Haider Abdul-Shafi, head of the Palestinian delegation at the Middle East Peace Conference in Madrid, Oct. 31, 1991)

The road to peace will be very long and it will be very difficult. We have to crawl before we can walk and we have to walk before we can run. Today, I think we all began to crawl. (James A. Baker III, Oct. 30, 1991)

Blessed are the peacemakers, for they will be called children of God. (Matthew 5:9, NRSV)

For more than a decade I have been taking an informal Middle East survey among active church members throughout the U.S. The results, though unscientific, are striking. The first question centers on what people think about a particular event, development, group, or scenario. The second question probes for another kind of perspective; it asks how to understand the particular event, development, group, or scenario within the broader Middle Eastern context. I find that most people have strong opinions about specific issues. I find remarkably few who can articulate a clear frame of reference within which to place the particular events about which they feel so vehemently.

The pattern is intriguing, but not too difficult to explain. For several decades, Americans have been inundated with media coverage of Middle Eastern events. This barrage of images and disjointed details is usually presented in relation to dramatic or sensational developments. News of a bomb incident or military clash—complete with graphic shots of the injured or dead—is sure to evoke a response; it does not necessarily translate into a coherent understanding of the dynamics at work.

Admittedly, the issues are many and sometimes complex. But they are not impenetrable. It is possible to begin to develop a frame of reference. The issue is not whether we can learn enough to make sense of the issues, but rather whether we care enough to invest the time and energy to learn. When something matters enough, most people will make it their business to learn what is minimally necessary for informed decisions. An example from the sphere of economics illustrates the point.

Few of us claim expertise in economics. Yet, economic realities are important for us all. Most of us, therefore, endeavor to know enough to make constructive decisions (or at least avoid harmful ones) about retirement plans, investments, buying and selling a home, and so forth. When we recognize that our understanding and perspectives inform decisions that directly affect our own economic well-being, we tend to take the issues seriously.

Although most Americans do not feel the impact personally or directly, what we say, do, and think about Middle East issues is extremely important. As citizens of the world's undisputed superpower, we bear a particular responsibility. The actions of our government—unlike those of Norway or Sri Lanka—have an immediate bearing on the daily lives of people throughout the Middle East. Whether we choose to become better informed and actively engaged in political processes or simply acquiesce to whatever is done in our name, we have made decisions. In a democracy we share in the processes of decision making.

The intense media focus precipitated by massive U.S. military involvement in the Middle East crisis of 1990–91 has created a "teachable moment." If we are prepared to think about and learn from these traumatic events, we can make considerable strides in developing a more accurate framework for understanding. The concerted efforts of individuals and groups can help raise the level of informed discussion within the society. It may also help create a political context in which U.S. government officials are more likely to pursue constructive peacemaking initiatives with the type of creativity and resolve demanded by the circumstances. Put another way, the "we" in President Bush's post-war promise ("No one will work harder than we will for peace and stability in the region."[1]) includes all of "us."

Sources of Frustration in the Middle East[2]

At any given time, turbulent developments are visible in different parts of the Middle East. These various dynamics are rooted in deep frustrations evident in unresolved local and re-gional problems. One or more such factors are often present in a particular setting. Understanding these dynamics helps make sense of the sometimes confusing behavior of people and groups. Four major sources of frustration are operative throughout the Middle East. All four were visible in relation to the 1991 Gulf war.

First, the region is plagued by complications stemming from a long history of foreign domination. For almost four centuries the Ottoman Turks ruled over the region. While they were Mus-lims, most Arabic-speaking Muslims and Christians perceived them as a foreign presence motivated by political ambition and visions of empire. The best interests of the indigenous population were not the primary concern of the Ottomans.

The complete dissolution of the already-fragmented Ottoman Empire after World War I shifted control of the Middle East to the colonial powers of Europe, most notably Great Britain and France. Many of the current problems in the region can be traced directly to policy decisions implemented by these colonial author-ities. New and frequently artificial boundaries were drawn divid-ing lands into areas under the European mandate; local rulers

---

1. Made on March 6, 1991.
2. A portion of this section is an expanded version of material first published in Charles A. Kimball, "The Case for Diplomacy: Settling Regional Disputes in an Interdependent World," *Sojourners* (Feb.-March, 1991), pp. 18–21.

were empowered in order to pursue the policies and interests of the colonial powers. The continuing fallout of these dynamics was plainly visible in the Gulf war.

Soon after the August 2, 1990, invasion of Kuwait, Saddam Hussein declared the territory the "19th province of Iraq." He spoke frequently of the artificial nature of Kuwait as a creation of the British. Although this rhetoric was designed to justify his actions, it was not without some merit. Kuwait did not exist prior to this century. It became a state in 1962. Ironically, the current Iraqi borders resulted from a piecing together of older Ottoman jurisdictions.

At a popular level, Saddam Hussein's statements appealed to the strong sense of inequity and inconsistency many people feel about the current configuration of nation-states. The borders do not always make sense in relation to natural divisions of people and geography. Saddam Hussein was far from consistent, however. The hypocrisy of the Iraqi leader's position became evident when the same issues he addressed vis-à-vis Kuwait were applied to the Kurdish people in his own country.

The Kurds are an identifiable people who number approximately twenty million. When the current boundaries were drawn after World War II, they were denied an earlier-promised independent territory in the region called Kurdistan. Rather, these non-Arab Sunni Muslims were divided into five other countries: the large majority reside in Turkey, Iran, and Iraq; smaller enclaves are found in Syria and the former U.S.S.R. What sense does this make? Not much. Yet, whenever the Kurds have sought to achieve a measure of autonomy, they have been brutally crushed.

During the early 1970s, Iraqi Kurds were encouraged to revolt and even supplied by the Shah of Iran. After the Shah fashioned a political deal with Iraq on other issues in 1975, however, Iran abandoned the Kurds. Then, as in the more widely covered chemical weapons assault of 1988, Kurdish rebels and non-combatant villagers were overwhelmed by the superior Iraqi army. Once again, in the aftermath of the Gulf war, Kurdish nationalists revolted against the oppressive policies of Saddam Hussein's regime. This time the international media covered the events. Reports and pictures depicting the widespread fighting and the plight of fleeing Kurdish refugees were grim. After two months of nonstop horror, Kurdish leaders reluctantly struck a deal when Saddam Hussein once again promised them limited autonomy.

Why would the Kurdish leaders trust the obviously untrustworthy Iraqi leader? They did not. Caught between the politics of various countries and with no hope of substantial external military assistance, they simply did not have other viable options. The Turkish government to the north, while somewhat helpful during the post-war Kurdish exodus, has a long history of persecuting its own Kurdish minority. Reports of Turkish government crackdowns on Kurds in both Turkey and Iraq during the fall of 1991 underscore the tenuous situation Kurds face.

Whatever the uneasy truce, few analysts imagine that this latest chapter will be the last in the tortured saga of the Iraqi Kurds. The whole process underscores the continuing importance of border and nation-state issues bequeathed by the colonialists.

A second major source of frustration derives from policies of unrepresentative governments. Currently, most Middle Eastern countries are ruled by autocratic military governments or monarchies. Few of these leaders came to power through democratic processes. Some assumed power under the hegemony of the colonial authorities; others seized power in military/political coups. The Emir of Kuwait and the King of Jordan represent the former; Saddam Hussein, Hafez al-Assad in Syria, and their respective Baathist ("Resurrection") parties represent the latter.

The lack of democracy and various freedoms, combined with appalling human rights abuses in many countries, deepens the frustration. People in the Middle East are like people everywhere. They rise in the morning, prepare children for school, work for a living when possible, worry about economic stresses and strains, visit the grandparents, and so forth. They want no less for themselves than people in Eastern Europe, Southern Africa, and Central America. Yet their basic human aspirations are often thwarted by forces they cannot control.

A closer look at Iraq helps bring these issues into sharp relief. Since 1979 Saddam Hussein has ruled Iraq as a tightly-controlled police state. The nature and extent of these repressive policies became public knowledge through numerous media reports following the invasion of Kuwait. The lack of options for those who opposed Saddam also became clear. Marching in the streets carrying a "down with Saddam" placard has not been an option. In fact, internal political debate has been curtailed to the point that publicly criticizing the Iraqi president is a capital offense.

In such a climate, dominant outside forces provide a convenient and politically acceptable target for popular discontent. In the case of Iraq, the United States and Israel—and subsequently those who linked up with them in the coalition against Iraq—served as the focus for Iraqi frustrations. Some anger vented on external powers is surely legitimate; much, however, derives from internal frustration that has no viable political outlet.

The extent of popular domestic frustration surfaced in the weeks following the Gulf war. Responding in part to the horrendous failure of Hussein's misguided policies and in part to President Bush's clarion call to rise up and overthrow "the dictator, Saddam," many Iraqis sought to topple the regime. The long-term outcome of the various conflicts—from the largely Shi'ite community supported by Iran in the South to the Kurdish Sunni population in the north—may not be clear for some years. Whatever the medium- and long-term results, the price will be high: many thousands of Iraqis have perished already in the popular revolts. Rhetoric from outside is easy; rising up against oppressive, brutal, and well-armed regimes on the inside clearly is not.

Serious human rights problems and the need for democratic reform are realities in Kuwait as well. Sorting out Kuwaiti internal dynamics will take time. The popular desire for substantial changes in post-war Kuwait was unmistakably clear in the early weeks after the liberation of this nation. Pressure from the populace forced the ruling family to promise democratic reforms, beginning with parliamentary elections in 1992. Exactly one year after the August 2, 1990, Iraqi invasion the *New York Times* featured a front-page story on the continuing nepotism, censorship, and lack of political freedom for women in Kuwait. The result of this return to the pre-war status quo was a pervasive depression and malaise. In fact, the situation in Kuwait worsened after the war. Tens of thousands of non-Kuwaiti Arabs have been forced to leave; thousands of *Biduns* (people without clear citizenship) who have lived their entire lives in Kuwait have been herded into makeshift refugee camps near the Iraqi border. In early 1992, the prospects for these people is anything but certain.

The precise future shape of Kuwaiti political structures remains to be seen. Other governments will face similar internal dynamics. From Saudi Arabia to Egypt to Algeria, the desire for reform and political change is present. No single pattern is discernible, however. Conservative Muslim groups, civil rights activists, women's organizations, and democratic reform parties form some of the most visible groups seeking change. In some settings political reform is inhibited by iron-fisted governmental policies; in other countries visible change may come quickly. The point to bear in mind is that frustrating internal dynamics create and feed political turbulence in different settings.

A third major dynamic stimulating unrest, also readily visible in the Gulf war, centers in the gross inequity in wealth and resources both within societies and between countries. The oil wealth controlled by the Saudi Arabian royal family, for instance, stands in stark contrast to the unspeakable poverty of most Egyptians just across the Red Sea. Other examples contrasting the "haves" and the "have nots" abound.

This disparity in resources, coupled with images of opulent lifestyles, breeds deep resentment. Western audiences caught glimpses of this following the war when the Emir of Kuwait delayed his return until a suitable place had been prepared for him. Many Kuwaitis, understandably, were not amused by their government's efforts to repair the Emir's palace before basic electric and water services were restored for the people who had endured seven months of Iraqi occupation and war. How much more the frustration when Kuwaiti leaders who had been in Saudi Arabia, London, or Paris, decide that many more non-Kuwaiti Arab residents must now leave the country. The rhetoric of "Arab solidarity," however convincing to the outside world, is often just that: rhetoric. The poorer cousins understandably resent hearing about Arab unity even as they experience blatant discrimination.

The fourth major source of frustration and instability in the Middle East derives from unresolved regional conflicts, most notably the half-century Israeli/Palestinian conflict and the longstanding, multi-sided civil war in Lebanon. The changing alliances and interplay among recognized governments and different non-governmental groups in the Middle East complicate the already intricate web of regional politics.

The interconnected nature of regional and global politics was readily apparent from the beginning of the Gulf crisis. Within hours of his military assault, Saddam Hussein came under intense and widespread regional and international pressure to withdraw from Kuwait. Leader after leader declared that such naked aggression must not be allowed to stand. Saddam Hussein's response moved at two levels. First, he sought to justify his actions in the context of the particular history of unresolved disputes between the two countries. The issues were real: they include border disputes and ownership of the islands of Warba and Bubiyan; alleged Kuwaiti exploitation of Iraq's Rumailah oil field; adherence to OPEC production quotas; and payments of loans incurred during Iraq's ten-year war with Iran. The points of dispute, however, did not justify the military takeover of Kuwait. Saddam Hussein also expressed willingness to withdraw if other occupying forces would do the same elsewhere in the Middle East. He called attention to the Israeli military occupation of the West Bank and Gaza since 1967 and the Syrian military deployment in Lebanon that dates to 1975. He challenged the international community with inconsistency in dealing with regional conflicts and military occupation. For many in the Middle East and elsewhere, Saddam Hussein's challenge hit home. In the fall of 1990, various diplomats—most notably the French, Soviet, and Yemeni representatives to the United Nations—floated plans that incorporated these concerns. Most included pledges for a UN-based Middle East regional peace conference as a carrot designed to induce Iraqi withdrawal from Kuwait. The U.S. vigorously opposed and effectively thwarted these approaches, arguing that such linkage would reward aggression and thus set a dangerous precedent. President Bush emphasized his view repeatedly: Iraq must withdraw from Kuwait unconditionally.

Official U.S. policy not withstanding, the pervasive interconnectedness of issues was evident on the ground in the Middle East. One vivid example of linkage involved Iraq's effort to draw Israel into the war by firing SCUD missiles at Israeli cities. Heavy U.S. diplomatic pressure and the rapid deployment of anti-SCUD Patriot missile defenses in Israel prevented swift Israeli retaliation. Hussein's strategy was transparent: he hoped to provoke a military response from Israel. Had Israel retaliated, the various Middle Eastern nations aligned with the Allied coalition would have been in an untenable position. They would have been perceived in Arab countries as joining arms with Israel and the U.S. to fight another Arab state. No one knows precisely how government leaders in Egypt, Saudi Arabia, or Syria would have reacted. Most analysts agreed, however, that these regimes would not have been able to ignore popular sentiment in their respective nations.

Saddam Hussein understood the political importance of the Israeli/Palestinian conflict as a regional issue. His actions sought both to deflect the focus off his invasion of Kuwait and rally political support by exploiting popular sentiment. Although Israel did not take the bait, the confrontation made clear the political reality of interconnected regional conflicts as a major source of instability in the Middle East. The entire episode underscored the urgent need for visible progress in the daunting search for peace and stability in this region.

The Difficult Road Toward Peace and Stability

One year after the formal end of the Gulf war, problems abound throughout the Middle East. Wherever you look, various sources of frustration are present. We have noted already some disturbing trends in Kuwait. In Iraq, the aftermath of war—from famine, disease, and severe economic dislocation, to complex political ambiguities—reveals a grim situation.

One horrific manifestation is seen in infant mortality rates. The *New York Times* reported on a public health study indicating the probable deaths of "tens of thousands" in Iraq's population of "more than three million children under five years old."[3] Lack

3. "Health Study Says Child Mortality Rate in Iraq Has Tripled," The *New York Times* (October 22, 1991), p. A6.

of clean water, continuing international sanctions, and civil strife were cited as the primary problems in the wake of the war. Even in the best-case scenario when the suffering is minimized, the long-term impact of these harsh realities will be destabilizing.

Syria, Egypt, and Jordan face severe economic problems as well as varying degrees of political unrest. On the positive side, these pressures and the changing patterns of geopolitical relations are pushing these governments toward new forms of cooperation and accommodation. While there are plenty of reasons for deep concern about the short- and middle-term prospects for this region, there are also reasons for hope. The most viable sign of hope in the aftermath of the Gulf war is found in the Israeli/Palestinian/Arab conflict.

President Bush underscored U.S. resolve to facilitate a Middle East peace process in an address to a joint session of Congress on March 6, 1991. Within days, Secretary of State James A. Baker III departed Washington on the first of eight extensive trips throughout the Middle East. Between March and August the different governments and parties to the conflict jockeyed for political position. Finally, after a series of alternately encouraging and discouraging developments, tangible signs of real progress began to surface.

The governments of Syria, Jordan, Lebanon, Saudi Arabia, Egypt, and Israel, respectively, declared their willingness to participate in a regional peace conference convened jointly by the U.S. and the U.S.S.R. The plan called for a brief, general conference of the participants (including official observers from the United Nations) followed by a series of bilateral negotiations between Israel and the various neighboring states. Parties on all sides of the conflict expressed guarded optimism as they referred to this initiative as an "historic chance for peace" in the turbulent region. Hopes for a negotiated settlement began to rise by August.

Even so, major problems remained unresolved. The most troublesome pre-negotiation issue centered on the composition of the Palestinian delegation. Israel refused to allow participation by any Palestinians associated with the Palestine Liberation Organization, exiled from the occupied territories or resident in East Jerusalem. Israel's position related, in part, to domestic political dynamics and, in part, to the projected outcome of the negotiation process. While Prime Minister Shamir did not want to be seen as the obstacle to peace, his longstanding rhetoric and the hardline position of the extreme right in Israel precluded a visible role for the PLO at the outset. The adamant rejection of East Jerusalem and diaspora Palestinians was designed to limit the concessions Israel would be asked to make. While the various Arab governments agreed with the PLO that these conditions were highly unfair, they also urged the Palestinians to compromise in order to get the negotiation process going.

The matter of Jerusalem is particularly sensitive. No issue is more volatile and controversial than the status of this ancient and unique city nestled in the Judean hills. Shamir and others have argued there is nothing to discuss concerning Jerusalem. The initial refusal to allow East Jerusalem Palestinians to participate directly related to this point. The Israelis feared that such participation might be interpreted as a tacit acknowledgment that Palestinians have legitimate claims to Jerusalem, claims that must be addressed in a comprehensive settlement.

In fact, there are many issues yet to be resolved about the status of Jerusalem. The original UN partition plan of 1947 called for a kind of international city, a *corpus separatum*, accessible to all. The official position of the U.S. government has been consistent since the 1940s: Jerusalem is disputed territory; the precise status of the city should be determined in the context of a comprehensive settlement. The Israelis vigorously disagree, arguing that Jerusalem, reunited in 1967, must remain the "eternal" capital of Israel. The depth of the religious and political attachments to this city was clear at the time of the 1978 Camp David Accords. While Menachem Begin and Anwar Sadat made many concessions, they did not find common ground on Jerusalem. In the end, Israel, Egypt, and the U.S. simply attached separate letters outlining their positions on Jerusalem to the Accords.

The issues related to Jerusalem and other disputed matters illustrated the difficulties to be overcome. Even so, the first major step toward the possible resolution of this longstanding conflict was taken in Madrid on October 30, 1991. There for the first time, Israelis and Arabs sat face-to-face at one table. For three intense days the various representatives put forth their positions on the nature of the problems and on the steps needed to move toward resolving them.

The primary elements of an Israeli/Palestinian peace settlement came more sharply into view during the historic days on Madrid. The Palestinians, who made enormous concessions to participate as a part of a joint Jordanian-Palestinian delegation, stressed several key points during the deliberations. The first three points are consistent with stated U.S. policies and long-established UN positions.

First, the Palestinians wanted assurances that all parties would enjoy the right to self-determination. Short of this, they accepted an initial acknowledgment of legitimate Palestinian political rights.

Second, they stressed the importance of UN Resolution 242 (adopted in 1967) as a basis for negotiation. This historic resolution establishes the "land for peace" formula. In 1988, the PLO formally accepted Res. 242 as a precondition to begin dialogue with the U.S. government. Further, "land for peace" was the central feature of the Israeli/Egyptian peace settlement in 1978.

Third, the Palestinians wanted assurances that the status of Jerusalem would be considered with the larger peace process.

In addition, the Palestinians underscored the need to address and resolve issues related to political and economic rights of Palestinians who now live outside the Occupied Territories. More than half of the five million Palestinians live outside of Israel and the Occupied Territories. Many live in refugee camps in Lebanon, Jordan, or Syria; others are dispersed throughout the Middle East, Europe, and North America. The status and rights of these people living in diaspora will be one of the most difficult matters to resolve.

Israel's stated priorities center on security, peaceful coexistence, and economic cooperation with the neighboring states. After decades of bitter strife, Israeli leaders are understandably wary of words. They have made clear repeatedly that they would not compromise at the point of Israel's physical security. The thrust of their position suggests a phased peace process in which Israel's perceived risks will be minimized. In the long run Israeli leaders—on the left and on the right of the political spectrum—desire peaceful and productive relations with the surrounding states.

Most analysts agree that a settlement will hinge on some type of "land for peace" arrangement. The most straightforward understanding is that Israel should trade the lands seized in the 1967 war (the West Bank, Gaza, and the Golan Heights) for a secure peace. Some modifications of these dividing lines no doubt will be required in order to meet security concerns. And, as suggested above, a phased process is most likely. Whether the Palestinians would choose ultimately to establish an independent state in the West Bank and Gaza or move into some type of confederation with Jordan (perhaps even with Israel one day) is not certain. But in principle, the Palestinians should have the right to exercise self-determination.

Any negotiation process surely will include numerous instances of political hardball, diversions, and setbacks. Not only do the conflicting parties have to deal each other, they all have complicated internal political factors to consider. These elements were clearly evident in the second round of Middle East peace talks, held in Washington, D.C. in mid-December 1991. After a five-day delay (precipitated by Israel's refusal to accept the U.S. terms for the time and place of the talks), the discussions began. Limited movement in bilateral talks with Syria and Lebanon was overshadowed by major procedural problems related to Palestinian representation. For three days, Israelis and Palestinians huddled in State Department hallways. The point of disagreement—the propriety of meeting directly outside the framework of the Jordanian-Palestinian delegation—effectively blocked significant progress. In the best-case scenario, negotiations will be slow and tedious. Extremist elements on all sides have made clear their opposition to compromise. Regrettably, we must expect some efforts to disrupt or shift the focus of negotiations. In the past, violent confrontations have all too often surfaced fears and thwarted potential progress. Anticipating such disruptions may help limit their impact.

New dynamics in the region provide the immediate impetus for movement toward a negotiated settlement. Alliances formed during the Gulf crisis have created new opportunities. The disintegration of the former U.S.S.R. has prompted several countries to move toward accommodation with Israel and better relations with the U.S. In addition, the Arabs who adopted a very hard line in support of Saddam Hussein's rhetoric have been forced to reassess their position in the wake of Iraq's humiliating military defeat.

In this setting, the role of the U.S. will be particularly crucial. As a strong ally of Israel, the U.S. can help address legitimate Israeli fears and security concerns even as it encourages flexibility and compromise. On the other hand, changing patterns of relations between the U.S. and key Arab states may also provide opportunities for constructive movement forward in the search for peace.

In the short term, several major obstacles can be removed in order to build trust. Three specific steps, among others, could prove to be particularly constructive. The first of these potentially helpful steps occurred when the United Nations General Assembly overwhelmingly overturned their 1975 "Zionism is racism" resolution. The two other actions depend more directly on the Arabs and Israelis themselves: Israel should halt its settlement process in the Occupied Territories, and the Arab states should lead the way in ending the longstanding economic boycott of Israel.

The second part of the Middle East peace process involves direct bilateral negotiations between Israel and the adjacent states. In addition to considering specific issues of mutual concern, the U.S. and Soviet/Russian sponsors hope these bilateral talks will feed into broader, long-term regional cooperation on vexing problems such as sharing the limited water resources and halting the burgeoning arms race.

Pursuing a viable Middle East peace process is the top priority in the wake of the traumatic Gulf war. The Israeli/Palestinian conflict is the most destabilizing factor in this strategically important and volatile region. Obviously, the road ahead is precarious. Trust between Middle Eastern adversaries falls somewhere between minimal and non-existent. At the same time, the prospects for genuine movement toward resolving this longstanding conflict are more hopeful than at any time during the past 25 years.

A durable peace between Israel and its Arab neighbors can bring hope and opportunity to millions of people who have lived in the shadow of fear and war for two generations. The commitment of leaders in the international community to facilitate the elusive search for peace is crucial. Even in the best-case scenario, however, an Israeli/Palestinian/Arab peace agreement will not provide a regional panacea. It will help by removing a pervasive and complicating factor in a region plagued with multiple problems and teeming with deep frustrations. Addressing the various sources of instability will require concerted efforts over time. While there are no easy answers or quick solutions, there are ways to move forward constructively. Political lessons from the Gulf crisis provide invaluable clues and indicators to guide this process.

Learning from the Gulf Crisis

The crisis in the Gulf demonstrated vividly the reality of global interdependence. On the eve of the twenty-first century, the world community is interlinked in unprecedented ways. Events in one part of the world are often directly relevant in many other places. In this instance, the issues raised by Iraq's actions in Kuwait could not be confined to a dispute between two nation-states. The political and economic shock of Iraq's invasion provoked a strong global response.

The Gulf crisis underscored both the necessity and possibility for broad-based cooperation in addressing regional and global problems. From the early days of the crisis, the United Nations was a primary arena for political activity. UN resolutions condemning the Iraqi aggression were followed by debates, decisions, and the imposition of punitive economic and political sanctions. The U.S. government played the major role, both within the UN and in the subsequent military response of the Allied coalition. Even so, the UN was revitalized as a valuable forum for decision-making and coordinated action in the international community.

In the aftermath of the war, the UN again has played a key role. UN peacekeeping forces were dispatched to buffer zones between Iraq and Kuwait in order to secure the ceasefire and provide stability for the understandably wary Kuwaitis. Multi-national forces under the UN flag also provided an invaluable presence in the largely Kurdish and Shi'ite regions, in the northern and southern portions of Iraq, respectively. In addition to physical security, the UN has served as an umbrella organization for international relief efforts directed to these Iraqi communities threatened by Saddam Hussein's regime. Finally, the UN remains the most effective global body equipped to assist refugees.

For several decades the UN has worked in the Middle East helping to meet human needs in conflict situations. Prominent examples include extensive work in Palestinian refugee camps (particularly in Gaza and the West Bank) under the auspices of the United Nations Relief and Works Agency, and peacekeeping forces since the mid-1970s in Lebanon and on the island nation of Cyprus. The UN was instrumental in the ceasefire and disengagement agreements ending the gruesome ten-year war between Iran and Iraq. In 1991 Javiar Perez de Cuellar, Secretary-General of the UN, played a key role in facilitating multi-lateral efforts to secure the release of Western hostages being held in Lebanon and Lebanese and Palestinians being held by Israel.

Many Middle East analysts are hopeful that the new Secretary-General, Butros Ghali, will continue to chart a constructive course toward peace and reconciliation. Ghali, who has been appointed to the top post for five years (1992–97), is well-equipped to facilitate Middle East peace. A Coptic Orthodox Christian, the seasoned diplomat has served for more than a decade as foreign minister in the predominantly Muslim country of Egypt. His direct involvement in the 1977–78 Egyptian/Israeli peace process could prove to be particularly valuable.

The need for an effective gathering point for the community of nations will continue to grow in coming years. While we live in a world of nation-states, many of the problems we face—from pollution of the air and oceans to conflict resolution—are problems that demand a cooperative, global response. The UN, which had been criticized severely and continually discredited during the tenure of Ronald Reagan, may offer the type of structure needed to address complex multi-national problems. In some instances, regional organizations (such as the Arab League or the European Economic Community or NATO) may provide the best vehicles to address multi-national issues. Whatever structures or organizations are deemed most helpful, this much is clear: the way forward in our increasingly fragile, interdependent world involves cooperative efforts that transcend traditional nation-state boundaries.

Another major lesson made clear by the Gulf crisis is found in the deep desire and need to change unrepresentative political structures. People in the Middle East observe the startling changes taking place in the new Commonwealth of Independent States (formerly the U.S.S.R.), Eastern Europe and South Africa. They, too, long for political freedom and democracy. The challenge for the U.S., the world's most powerful nation, and other countries involves finding ways to encourage political reform and the growth of democracy in the Arab world. The time is right. U.S. influence in the post-war era is substantial.

The U.S. government is committed ideologically to democracy and the principle of self-determination of indigenous people. This is not the same, however, as political and economic support for the process of change. Democracy is a messy business. It is far less predictable than a military government or dynastic regime headed by a monarch. If people are free to express themselves in a democracy, the precise contours of the political landscape cannot be known in advance. Some of the short- and medium-term consequences of democracy in the Middle East may well undercut U.S. influence in the region. Shi'ites in Iraq, for instance, may choose a type of Islamic government aligned with Iran. In the long run, however, strong U.S. support for the principles of free choice and democracy will enhance relationships in the community of nations.

Conversely, a failure to support the very democratic principles Americans espouse will have adverse consequences. In its relationships in the Arab world, the U.S. government must not appear lukewarm on democracy. It must avoid the hypocrisy of talking about democracy, political freedom, and self-determination while, at the same time, supporting repressive regimes that deny those rights. Policy decisions must not center on perceived short-

65

term interests to the exclusion of principled bases for political reform. Careful scrutiny of U.S. policy decisions related to Iraq (or Iran or Lebanon, for that matter) between 1975 and 1991 illustrates the point.

Strong U.S. opposition to Iran encouraged support for Iraq in the 1980s. The rationale, "the enemy of my enemy is my friend," inevitably leads to all sorts of unlikely alliances. This is a dangerous and potentially counter-productive basis for policy decisions. The perceived short-term interests used to justify substantial support for Saddam Hussein's repressive regime prior to August of 1990 pale by comparison to the longer-term consequences of not opposing such tyranny. We need to remember that these tactics were not new. Saddam Hussein had employed these and similar methods repeatedly during the ten-year war with neighboring Iran. During those years, when Hussein enjoyed political, economic, and military support from the U.S. and many others in the Allied coalition, Iraq frequently fired SCUD missiles (with much larger explosives) into Iranian cities. Iraq also deliberately dumped crude oil into the Gulf for perceived military advantage. Further, Hussein did what was only feared in the 1991 war: he ordered the use of chemical weapons against Iranian soldiers and Iraqi Kurdish civilians. Where was the outcry prior to August 1990? The response of the world community to Iraq's behavior was remarkably muted in 1987 and 1988.

We all need to do some serious soul-searching at this point. Righteous indignation in 1990–91 raises hard questions about our moral vacillation. Why was our concern for human suffering so selective? Why did Western powers cynically supply both Iran and Iraq in their dreadful ten-year war that cost a million lives? How can our governments supply repressive regimes in some settings and denounce repressive regimes with moral indignation in other settings? What are our responsibilities as citizens to understand and respond to these patterns of behavior?

What have we learned through the Gulf crisis? People throughout the Middle East will be watching and weighing carefully the rhetoric and behavior of the U.S. government as the unquestioned leader of the community of nations.

The two most troubling conflicts in the region provide urgent opportunities to encourage democratic change. A major obstacle to peace in the fifteen-year-old Lebanese conflict centers on this issue. The need for political reform is at the heart of the multi-sided civil war in this beautiful and tragic land. The system of representation by confessional group is now long out of step with the demographic realities present when the French colonial rulers established the government structure based on the census of 1932.

Currently, there are hopeful signs that the Lebanese may be ending the destructive factional fighting and progressing toward new, more democratic and equitable political structures. The long-overdue release of Anglican envoy Terry Waite, the Beirut-based AP bureau chief Terry Anderson, and other Western hostages in the fall of 1991 is one such hopeful sign. After holding these hostages captive for as long as six years, extremist factions in Lebanon were persuaded finally to end this deplorable chapter in Lebanese history and help to chart a new course in their divided nation.

Leaders in the community of nations should seize this moment and facilitate the process. Because of its uniquely diverse population, Lebanon is a kind of microcosm of the Middle East. Assisting this nation in its efforts to rebuild a multi-religious society in a way that enshrines democratic principles and respects the rights of all communities is a top priority. Lebanon may yet emerge from its devastating civil war and become a model for diverse societies in an interdependent world. If the Lebanese cannot find new ways to live together with their pluralism, it will bode well neither for the Middle East nor for the rest of us who share a pluralistic world.

The Israeli/Palestinian conflict also presents opportunities to foster democratic structures. At every phase of the peace process, the Palestinians should be encouraged and assisted in implementing elections and other democratic means to identify their leaders and representatives and to express their national will. Whatever political configuration results from the negotiations, Israelis and Palestinians have both the right and the opportunity to pursue self-determination through democratic processes. Efforts to negotiate with unrepresentative leaders, impose decisions, or dictate undemocratic political structures are doomed to fail in the short and long run.

Another critical lesson from the Gulf crisis is found beyond the headlines. Understandably, most media attention focuses on breaking news stories such as the daily combat statistics from the front lines or developments in the peace process or negotiations for hostages. Thoughtful attention to such developments is both appropriate and necessary. But, as we have seen above, the sources of instability are many. Any real hope for a more positive future in the Middle East requires concerted efforts to address these sources of frustration. Visible concern and support for pressing human interests is critical. Humanitarian assistance for people in need and political support to safeguard human rights are two crucial components in the mix.

Widespread human suffering is a harsh reality in the Middle East. The lack of food, adequate shelter, clean water, medical care, and sanitation take a heavy toll. Many of these problems arise in conflict situations or when refugees are displaced; many basic needs go unmet because of rampant poverty spreading in the shadow of unimaginable wealth. The U.S. and other prosperous nations should lead the way in humanitarian assistance. Demonstrable concern for the well-being of people caught in circumstances they cannot control is not only morally required, it will help prevent short-sighted and blatantly self-serving policy decisions that tend to overlook the human realities on the ground. The massive U.S. response to the plight of Kurdish refugees fleeing Iraq's army, though slow to develop, exemplifies the importance of this factor. Humanitarian efforts must go beyond charity. We must seek to understand the causes of economic inequity and assess our complicity in the process.

Finally, long-term support for fundamental human rights should inform policy decisions in visible ways. Prior to and throughout the Gulf war, President Bush championed the cause of human rights while promising to halt naked aggression and tyranny. He took the moral high ground. In early January 1991, the President justified the move toward war by citing an Amnesty International report on Iraq. In a television interview broadcast on network television, he said the following:

It should be compulsory reading for all of those who say "that's someone else's problem, that's halfway around the world." The brutality, the rape, the pillage, the plunder—with case histories to back it up—is appalling.

President Bush later called the Amnesty reports "sickening." Without question, he was correct. They were sickening. Horrified by the despicable human rights abuses, many Americans readily accepted the President's rationale for war. Many elsewhere in the world doubted the sincerity of the rationale. The questions people now ask are these: How strong is the commitment to safeguarding human rights? How selective was Mr. Bush's dismay? Will Bush and other leaders read and act on Amnesty reports detailing similar sickening abuses elsewhere in the world? Will the resolve to halt tyranny and reverse aggression go beyond lip service when oil is not a central factor in the equation?

The issue is one of consistency. The strength and quality of U.S. leadership relates directly to the way our government stands up for human interests. In the Middle East, this will mean unambiguous clarity in opposition to human rights violations. The message must be the same for close allies like Israel, whose various human rights violations are well-documented by the U.S. State Department, as well as for uneasy "coalition partners" like Syria, whose brutally repressive policies rival those of Iraq. Positive leadership by the U.S. government requires that U.S. policies and behavior be consistent with its rhetoric.

There are no easy answers in the Middle Eastern political arena. However, focused attention on human interests and consistent support for democratic principles provide a sound framework within which to develop policies. The importance of identifiable and principled political positions is crucial in light of the other major dynamics operative in this region. We have already explored the sometimes turbulent religious developments in the region. We turn next to a consideration of oil and related economic factors as we seek to understand the major components producing the volatile mix in the Middle East.

CHAPTER 3

Oil

"No blood for oil!" (A popular chant among many anti-war protesters)

"Our jobs, our way of life, our own freedom and the freedom of friendly countries around the world would suffer if control of the world's great oil reserves fell into the hands of Saddam Hussein." (George Bush, August 15, 1990)

"One who puts on armor should not brag like one who takes it off." (II Kings 20:11 NRSV)

Iraq's invasion of Kuwait provoked a swift and strong outcry from much of the world community. This act of naked aggression sent shock waves through every nation dependent upon the oil produced in the Persian/Arabian Gulf. Within hours of Iraq's military takeover, world oil prices began to rise rapidly in anticipation of diminishing supply. At the same time, stock markets from Tokyo to London and New York plummeted in the face of economic uncertainty. One did not need an advanced degree in economics to perceive that these turbulent events in two major oil producing states—Iraq and Kuwait—were intimately linked to global economic structures.

With the capture of Kuwait, Saddam Hussein controlled approximately 20% of OPEC's production and 25% of the world's known oil reserves. No sooner than analysts began appearing on network news programs to speculate on the possible economic and political consequences, an even more ominous scenario surfaced. Perhaps Saddam Hussein would not stop at the borders of Kuwait. Perhaps he had designs on an even larger prize: the oil fields of Saudi Arabia. The fear of further military aggression was emphasized in the initial U.S.-led military response. Within one week of the Iraqi invasion, President Bush announced that he was dispatching the U.S. military in order to thwart any further advance by Iraq. Thus, Operation Desert Shield, an ostensibly defensive action, was born.

The pace of events quickened through the fall of 1990. In the political arena, increasingly strong rhetoric was audible in many quarters. At the same time, both the Iraqi and the Allied military forces in and around Kuwait continued to grow. By the time Desert Shield became Desert Storm in January 1991, more than one million people were deployed in the shifting sands of the Middle Eastern desert.

As we noted in the introduction above, few people in the West offered any brief in support of the policies of Saddam Hussein. The debates turned not on whether to oppose Iraq's aggression, but on how best to stop and reverse it. Many in North America and Europe were deeply troubled by and visibly opposed to the seemingly unswerving march toward war. Ten of thousands of people gathered in New York, San Francisco, Washington, Paris, Frankfort, and Rome to voice their opposition to a military confrontation. "No blood for oil!" was, perhaps, the most popular and widespread slogan employed by the Western anti-war protesters. In view of the various scenarios depicting a potential cataclysm, the chant struck a nerve.

In addition to the slogans of protesters, many prominent figures sought to highlight this truth. South Carolina Senator Ernest Hollings strongly and consistently opposed the military policy. On several occasions, he repeated his view: "All the oil in Kuwait is not worth the life of one American G.I." True enough. How can one ever put a monetary price on the value of human life?

As hundreds of thousands of Americans departed for the Middle East, local and national news programs featured stories of families traumatized by impending separation and the prospects for war. How many of these soldiers would not return to their families? Richard Murphy, former Undersecretary of State for the Near East, reported the consensus view in early November to a large gathering of Middle East scholars meeting in San Antonio. Reflecting on factors that might inhibit a U.S. military offensive, he told those in attendance: "The Pentagon estimates some 25,000 to 30,000 American casualties minimum in the event full-scale ground fighting occurs." He then conceded that the Bush administration recognized how difficult it would be to "sustain popular support" for its military approach should the American casualties reach these levels. The calculating, matter-of-fact tone of the discourse was chilling.

What precisely were these people being asked to fight and possibly die for? Was this the beginning of another ambiguous and prolonged conflict like Vietnam? U.S. leaders offered several arguments in support of the government's military policies. Two weeks after the crisis began, President Bush clearly stated his perception of the major issues at stake in these dramatic developments. In the quotation cited at the beginning of this chapter, Mr. Bush stressed that "our jobs, our way of life, our own freedom . . . would suffer if the world's great oil reserves fell into the hands of Saddam Hussein."

Soon, however, the economic arguments gave way to other concerns advanced to support the Allied position. The most frequent justification centered on the tyranny and brutality of Saddam Hussein. He was portrayed as the new Hitler, a ruthless character whose oppressive policies must be stopped before they spread further. Bush declared repeatedly, "Saddam Hussein's aggression against Kuwait will not be allowed to stand." This theme, illustrated with vivid accounts of widespread human rights abuses in Kuwait documented by Amnesty International and others pulled at the emotional heartstrings of most Americans. The appeal was successful. While few people were prepared to fight and die for fossil fuels or to protect "our way of life" by keeping the price of oil stable, the image of a new Hitler commanding a massive army was compelling.

Without question, the issues converging in the Gulf were partly about tyranny, human rights, and freedom. But these were not the primary factors motivating the massive military response to Saddam Hussein. There are many brutal, ruthless leaders whose behavior evokes and sometimes warrants comparison with Hitler. Whatever the public rhetoric, this much is clear: The crisis in the Gulf revolved first and foremost around oil and economic interdependence.

Ross Perot, the billionaire Texas businessman who opposed an offensive military option, called for a more honest and straight-forward examination of the U.S. "interests" driving the risky policy decisions. He reminded American audiences that the U.S. had enormous economic leverage with Saddam Hussein. Saddam may control the oil, but it is of little value unless he can sell it. In retrospect, it is clear that the impetus driving the Allied response to the Gulf crisis cannot be reduced to a principle upholding the sanctity of nation-states or moral outrage over brutally repressive policies. Neither can the global dependence on oil and the broad-er pattern of economic interdependence be dismissed sim-plistically with a slogan. The Gulf war illustrated forcefully the interconnectedness of these complex issues. It also reminded us all of the precarious dynamics tied to our dependence on fossil fuels.

The Politics of Oil

Oil stands at the center of a vast and complex web of intercon-nected global economic structures. In the view of best-selling author Daniel Yergin, oil is the "prize" that has shaped political and economic behavior throughout the twentieth century. His 900-page book published in early 1991, *The Prize: The Epic Quest for Oil, Money and Power*, documents this assertion. Yergin traces the critical role of oil through numerous world events—from Winston Churchill's decision to convert British naval forces from coal to oil prior to World War I to the 1953 U.S.-led coup restoring the Shah to power in Iran and the more recent machinations of OPEC. His detailed study explores three great themes that under-lie the story of oil:

The first is the rise and development of capitalism and modern business. Oil is the world's biggest and most pervasive business, the greatest of the great industries that arose in the last decades of the nineteenth century. . . . Today, oil is the only commodity whose doings and controversies are to be found regularly not only on the business page but also on the front page. . . . The second theme is that of oil as a commodity intimately intertwined with national strategies and global politics and power. . . . A third theme in the history of oil illuminates how ours has become a "Hydrocarbon Society." . . . [1]

The consequences of catastrophic and far-reaching economic dislocation related to instability in global oil markets are quite real. Two major events in the 1970s illustrate the political and economic importance of oil worldwide.

In 1973–74, oil prices increased four-fold. The 1973 Arab-Israeli war precipitated an Arab oil embargo. Most Americans remember sitting in long lines at gas stations and paying substantially more for gasoline during and after the embargo. We don't recall as readily the wider economic developments at the time. Coming when worldwide demand was high and reserves were depleted, the embargo stimulated frenzied speculative buying. The rapid rise in oil prices triggered a recession throughout much of the world. The demand for oil decreased until industrialized economies began to recover later in the decade.

The second price shock of the decade came in 1979 in response to the Iranian revolution. Iran, one of the world's largest producers of oil, decreased production during the revolution. The shortage, accompanied by fears of further price increases, stimulated a new wave of panic buying on global spot markets. The price of oil doubled in the process. Once again, the industrialized world experienced a major economic downturn in response to the shock of higher oil prices.

President Carter's urgent plea for voluntary conservation and a diversified energy policy was consistent with the events of the day and in view of longer term prospects. His calls for austerity and lowered expectations were not popular politically. By the

1. Daniel Yergin, *The Prize: The Epic Quest for Oil, Money and Power* (New York: Simon and Schuster, 1991), pp. 13–14.

early 1980s, however, the dehabilitating oil-related economic events of the 1970s were fading from memory. Unlimited prosperity became a watchword during the Reagan presidency. Whatever the public posture, economic realities and the politics of oil were well known in the corridors of power.

In 1985, Thomas McNaugher of the Brookings Institution published a book articulating a strategy for protecting U.S. security and economic interests in the Persian Gulf. Written during a worldwide oil glut, the book, *Arms and Oil: U.S. Military Strategy and the Persian Gulf,* leaves no doubt about the global importance of oil in the Gulf region. Read through the lens of the Gulf crisis, his views take on an added poignancy:

> Several factors make it probable that oil will regain its critical importance to the world's economy, and that Persian Gulf states will actually increase in importance as time goes by. . . .
>
> Oil is the world's residual energy source; swings in its price affect all energy markets. . . . The adage that U.S. allies like France and Japan should be held relatively more responsible for security around the Persian Gulf because so much of their oil comes from the Gulf misses the mark when it comes to oil and energy markets. Supply cuts among Gulf producers would force Japan and France to seek oil in other markets, bidding up its price to everyone.
>
> The political importance of oil derives from the effects of changes, or feared changes, in its price. Earlier shocks introduced a host of domestic political problems for oil-consuming states—inflation, recession, dislocations within the labor force, and unemployment.[2]

The economic shocks from the 1990–91 Gulf crisis are far-reaching. They already have produced "a host of domestic problems for oil-consuming states." A full analysis of the consequences may not be possible for several years. Even so, some of the short-term effects are already clear. In the U.S., several major airlines were crippled by the sudden combination of higher fuel costs and fewer passengers (due in part to fears of terrorism). The entire economy in North America moved deeper into recession as various industries—from the manufacture and sale of automobiles to the travel and resort businesses—experienced significant

2. Thomas L. McNaugher, *Arms and Oil: U.S. Military Strategy and the Persian Gulf* (Washington, D.C.: The Brookings Institution, 1985), pp. 6–9.

slowdowns. Economic uncertainty was evident throughout the marketplace as consumer spending on non-essential items slowed markedly. By Christmas 1991, even the most optimistic economic pundits in the Bush Administration acknowledged that the country was in a recession.

Far less visible, but often far more devastating were (and are) the economic hardships experienced by many developing countries. Most are highly dependent upon imported oil and therefore highly vulnerable. The shaky, debt-burdened economies of most developing nations are among the least able to absorb abrupt increases in the cost of petroleum.

In many lands, such as Egypt, India, Pakistan, Bangladesh, Yemen, Sri Lanka, and the Philippines, another economic blow is now being felt. For years a virtual army of laborers and domestic workers have lived and worked in the oil-producing Gulf states. Their productivity abroad annually infused many millions of dollars in remittances back into their own countries. The hard currency thus earned helped both to support extended families and to stimulate generally weak economies. In the crisis, the vast majority of expatriate workers fled as refugees. Not only were they forced to leave most of their possessions behind, but they returned to their home countries, where many now sit idle.

The severity of this situation was spelled out in the headline of a full-page article in the *New York Times* published four months after the war: "Displaced in the Gulf War: Five Million Refugees" (Sunday, June 16, 1991). The article presented startling information. Officials in Bangladesh, for instance, estimated that 110,000 Bangladeshi citizens working in Iraq and Kuwait before the war supported over one million dependents in Bangaldesh by sending home some $50 million dollars each year. In Pakistan, the numbers were even more dramatic. The 160,000 Pakistanis who fled Iraq and Kuwait had been putting between $150 and $200 million into the economy of Pakistan through transfers to dependents at home.

Western media coverage of fleeing refugees concentrated before the war on the tens of thousands stranded at the Iraqi-Jordanian border. After the war, the attention centered on emergency relief efforts for Kurdish refugees fleeing toward Turkey and Iran. Without question, the media visibility aroused public opinion which, in turn, forced a U.S.-led humanitarian response. These massive efforts helped avert short-term disaster for many people. But, the problems are far from over. The human misery caused by widespread economic dislocation over the long term is all too real even if they are much less visible in the Western media.

The pervasive influence of oil reaches into every corner of the world. This influence is most conspicuous, however, in the largest consumer nation: the United States of America. A closer look at patterns of consumption is instructive. It makes clear why oil resources in the Gulf have been so central in the shaping of U.S. political and military policy. At the same time, it challenges us to learn from the traumatic events of the Gulf crisis and to reassess elements of "our way of life" that can be modified for the benefit of all.

The Growing Dependence on Oil

Daniel Yergin describes succinctly North Americans' massive dependence on oil:

> Today, we are so dependent on oil, and oil is so embedded in our daily doings, that we hardly stop to comprehend its pervasive significance. It is oil that makes possible where we live, how we live, how we commute to work, how we travel—even where we conduct our courtships. It is the lifeblood of suburban communities. Oil (and natural gas) are the essential components in the fertilizer on which world agriculture depends; oil makes it possible to transport food to the totally non-self-sufficient megacities of the world. Oil also provides the plastics and chemicals that are the bricks and mortar of contemporary civilization.[3]

With a moment's reflection, the profound truth of Yergin's statement begins to sink in. I first read these words while sitting at my desk in the study at home. Glancing around the room, I counted more than fifty items that obviously use plastic, including: the telephone, computer, discs, printer, TV, radio/CD play-

---

3. Yergin, p. 14.

er, video and cassette tapes and holders, notebooks, desk orga-
nizer, various pens and highlighters, Swiss Army knife, the handle
on scissors, two clocks, calculator, notecard holders, correction
fluid "bottles"—even my souvenir cups from golf tournaments,
football games, and Disney World. The list goes on and on.

This visual tour of the "plastic things" in my study was striking.
We rarely stop to consider how many common items are linked
to petroleum. The experience also conjured up an image from the
classic scene at the beginning of the 1960s film *The Graduate*.
Dustin Hoffman, the new college grad, was pulled aside at his
party for some sage advice upon which he might build his future.
"Just one word," he was told in a whisper reserved for conveying
inside information, " . . . Plastics!" "Plastics?" asked Hoffman.
"Plastics," was the reply. A quarter-century later, it appears Dustin
Hoffman was given solid advice. The rapid increase in consumption of plastics was noted in a CNN factoid (a tidbit of information
flashed on the screen between news segments) in August of 1991:
"Americans use 21 times more plastic today than in 1951." From
the vantage point of the desk in my study, that seems a conservative figure.

When we widen the circle to consider the vast transportation
and agricultural networks and the extensive role of chemicals in
our society, Yergin's thesis is all the more compelling. Oil, more
than any other commodity, is at the center of the U.S. economic
structure. Predictably, seven of the top twenty companies on the
Fortune 500 list are oil companies. A large percentage of the
petroleum consumed, however, is imported. This dependency
upon imported oil creates potential instability and vulnerability
in the entire economic structure.

Events in the 1970s encouraged concerted efforts to pursue a
long-term plan leading toward energy self-sufficiency. Considerable progress was achieved in the decade between 1974 and 1985.
Intentional efforts at energy conservation and improved efficiency reduced consumption substantially. U.S. oil imports fell
from a high of nine million barrels per day (b.p.d.) in 1978 to five
million b.p.d. in 1985. In the five-year period 1985–1990, however, the patterns reversed. In 1990, the U.S. imported over eight
million b.p.d., once again approaching the record levels of 1978.

These figures, combined with a decline in U.S. production during the 1980s, result in an even higher level of dependence on imported oil. In 1990, imported oil accounted for more than 40% of the oil consumed in the U.S. If current patterns of consumption continue, the picture is not likely to improve; rather, it will almost certainly worsen.

Consumption will be a central factor in shaping energy policies for the future. Currently, the U.S. per capita consumption rates are nearly twice as high as those in the industrialized countries of Europe and Japan. As inexpensive domestic energy sources decline, the need for imported oil will rise. So, too, will the U.S. economy be increasingly vulnerable to price shocks and fluctuations emanating from the major oil-producing states, most notably the Persian/Arabian Gulf where two-thirds of the world's known oil reserves are located.

President Bush wasn't joking when he warned that "our way of life" was threatened by Saddam Hussein's control of the oil under Iraq and Kuwait. The direct and forceful effort to evict Iraqi forces from Kuwait represented one approach to the problem. In broad economic terms, the policy was informed by the desire to assure a steady and dependable supply of oil for the West. There are, of course, diplomatic ways to speak about this need for access to oil. Rather than a straightforward and crass declaration that we want and need the oil produced in the Gulf, political leaders speak instead in more euphemistic terms about "protecting our vital interests."

In the current scheme of things, petroleum is vital to the United States—economically, politically, militarily. Even so, proclaiming the oil in another region to be "our vital interests" is presumptuous, particularly when one considers the clear commitment to use military force to "protect" these "interests." Imagine a scenario in which the government of Bangladesh or Ethiopia declared the wheat in Kansas to be their "vital interests." The fact that the wheat belongs to the farmers in Kansas does not lessen Bangladesh or Ethiopia's need for bread just to survive physically. In order to protect their "vital interests," they deploy naval forces in the Gulf of Mexico and seek military bases in the region. They then declare their readiness to use force if anyone threatens access to the wheat.

Like most analogies, this one breaks down when it is pushed. The scenarios are not parallel. The issue of meeting a particular need, however urgent, is complicated by international economic structures and geopolitical realities. Nevertheless, it is instructive to ponder the example. How would such action appear to others in the world of nation-states? How much more striking the scenario if Bangladesh or Ethiopia were places where people already had an abundance of wheat in relation to the rest of the world!

The U.S. concern for a steady external supply of petroleum is one side of the economic equation. The other side focuses on demand. Viewed from this angle, our U.S. dependence is due in large part to the consumption levels inherent in "our way of life." Changes in current patterns are required. There are many ways to reduce demand, including conservation, improving energy efficiency, and the development of alternative sources of energy. Concerted efforts in all of these areas will be necessary if the U.S. hopes to reduce its growing dependence on imported oil.

Poised on the brink of a new millennium, the situation requires that we in the West face this reality squarely. Decreasing consumption is in both our own self interest and the interests of other nations which need imported oil. Vigorous efforts to understand the operative dynamics and cooperatively to explore ways to defuse the ticking bomb are urgently needed. Complacency and miscalculations about global stability can have far-reaching consequences, particularly in an interdependent world that is armed to the teeth. Nowhere are the issues more sharply focused than in the Middle East where vast oil reserves feed an escalating arms race in the midst of political instability.

The Middle East Arms Race

Among the most sobering discoveries of the Gulf war were those related to the proliferation of diverse and deadly weapons systems. The burgeoning international arms industry thrives in the Middle East. Per capita, the nations in this strategically important region are the most heavily armed in the world. For the many Westerners who had simply not paid much attention to the massive sales and transfers of arms, the Gulf crisis and war provided a disconcerting wake-up call.

The growth in Middle Eastern arms sales and the proliferation of weapons systems during the past three decades is mind-boggling. The percentage in military expenditures for many Middle Eastern nations increases every year. Military sales remain a very lucrative business, one in which billions of dollars change hands every year. On March 7, 1990, just over one week after the conclusion of the Gulf war, National Public Radio reported some startling statistics about the "arm sales heaven" in the Middle East: between 1982 and 1989 Saudi Arabia and Iraq spent $44 and $43 billion on weapons, respectively; six Middle Eastern nations account for one-half of all arms sales in the world; and the 1990 report to Congress indicated that U.S. arms sales to the Middle East that year ($33 billion) represented two-thirds of total foreign sales.

These staggering expenditures on armaments often come at the expense of much-needed social and economic modernization. The 1989 report by the American Friends Service Committee, *A Compassionate Peace*, highlights the cost of militarization in this region:

> In the Middle East plowshares are being beaten into swords. The military has the largest work force and is the predominant employer of those with education; it is the leading employer in urban areas. For the region as a whole, approximately 16 percent of the gross national product (GNP) is spent on the military; the figure is considerably higher in Syria, Israel, Iran, and Iraq, where an average of about 26 percent of all government expenditures is for the military.[4]

During the Gulf crisis, we learned that Iraq, a country many North Americans had trouble locating on a map prior to August of 1990, was pre-eminent in the Middle East arms bazaar. The dangers posed by a militarily strong despot like Saddam Hussein

4. Everett Mendelsohn, *A Compassionate Peace: A Future for Israel, Palestine, and the Middle East* (New York: Hill and Wang, 2nd rev. ed., 1989), p. 147.

suddenly became clear. Most Westerners were simply unaware that Iraq, a nation of 18 million, maintained a standing army of more than one million. In addition to "conventional" weapons—tanks, jet fighters, land mines, etc.—Iraq possessed scores of Soviet-made SCUD missiles that were capable of hitting targets hundreds of miles away. Chemical weapons were also part of the arsenal. Striking pictures from the Middle East left no doubt about Iraq's deadly capability: prior to the war U.S. Marines explained to television audiences how necessary and how uncomfortable their chemical warfare suits were in the desert heat; Western journalists filed reports wearing gas masks as air raid sirens warned of incoming missiles; Israelis were rarely seen without their government-issued gas masks.

But, that was not all. Considerable speculation centered on how advanced Iraq's biological and nuclear weapons were. Serious questions surfaced, but straightforward answers were hard to find. What might Saddam Hussein do with biological agents? Where might his operatives use them? Just how close was Iraq to developing a nuclear device? Who else had or was seeking to obtain weapons of mass destruction? A broad, international consensus affirmed that the situation was intolerable.

In the months after the war, a series of UN inspection teams discovered more precisely the nature and extent of Iraq's diverse arsenal. Saddam Hussein, they reported, was seeking to develop a nuclear weapon through four different programs, some phases of which were far more advanced than had been thought. They also located and oversaw the dismantling of Iraq's "super gun" project. Once operational, this gigantic canon would have been capable of firing artillery shells (potentially equipped with chemical or biological agents) at targets as far away as Tehran, Damascus, Tel Aviv, and Cairo.

Behind the lament over this precarious state of affairs, other questions also began to be asked. How did Iraq achieve this level of military sophistication? Who armed this "new Hitler"? What safeguards can prevent juntas or individual leaders from obtaining whatever weapons they want? Is a fat checkbook the only prerequisite for procuring virtually any type of weapon?

These and related questions are anything but rhetorical. After the Gulf war, we learned that the U.S., the former U.S.S.R., France, Great Britain, the People's Republic of China, and many other nations had sold Iraq billions of dollars of weaponry in the 1980s.[5] In addition, German companies were implicated for their assistance in developing Iraq's chemical weapons capability. Furthermore, another economic power, Japan, was in on the act as well. Japanese firms were instrumental in designing and building deep, sophisticated bunker systems for Iraq. Saddam Hussein personally enjoyed the safety of a network of bunkers capable of withstanding a nuclear blast. Scores of other bunkers were constructed for troops, storage of weapons, and military aircraft. "Defense" is a lucrative business; the general public in the West discovered just how lucrative it is when we learned how the various supplier nations repeatedly clamored to get a piece of the pie.

Deep concern over the volatile mixture of petrodollars, massive accumulations of weapons, and political instability did not begin in 1990, however. A decade before Iraq's invasion of Kuwait, various organizations warned of dire consequences if these dangerous trends continued unchecked. In 1980, for example, the National Council of Churches' Governing Board addressed these very concerns in its "Middle East Policy Statement." The detailed document, adopted after a two and one-half year study process, framed the issues with these prophetic words:

> The recent acquisition of great national wealth through increased oil income has created a lucrative market for arms sales. In this context, the temptation to offset balance of payments deficits by means of arms sales is strong. . . . The United States alone is not at fault. Other arms producing nations, both East and West, compete for influence in the region by supplying arms and military training. Superpower rivalries, ideological conflict and maneuvering to assure oil supplies or strategic advantage lead to outside interference in the internal affairs of Middle Eastern states. Transnational corporations seek to influence government policies in their own interest and these tendencies are exacerbated by unprecedented wealth through petrodollars. All these factors, many of them in

5. A front page article in the *New York Times*, "U.S. Secretly Gave Aid to Iraq Early in Its War against Iran" (Jan. 26, 1992), reported that the U.S. government provided "arms, technology, and highly classified intelligence" to Iraq beginning in 1982.

conflict, create destabilization and slow efforts to improve the quality of life of its people.[6]

In a word, we all are implicated in the problem. For four decades, the U.S. has used arms exports to the Middle East as a way to strengthen governments perceived to be friendly to U.S. political, strategic, and economic interests. Flooding the Middle East region with expensive, sophisticated weapons may make sense in the context of short-term economic gain. Analysts and strategic planners can sometimes make a strong case for limited political benefits associated with providing weaponry. In the long run, however, such self-serving behavior is bound to be counterproductive. It puts much of the world at risk. No one can measure accurately the negative effect it has on the populace of these highly militarized societies. Moreover, no one can presume to control the fluid movement or use of armaments in a region where alliances are constantly changing. Two examples from highly publicized international events underscore the sinister and pervasive nature of this problem.

During the 1979–81 Iranian hostage crisis, President Carter sought to impose a total economic and military blockade on Iran. He invoked the Emergency International Economic Powers Act for the first time since its inception. Under the provisions of this law, any U.S. citizen or corporation doing business with Iran was subject to felony prosecution of up to ten years imprisonment and a $50,000 fine. I knew well these strictures since I was involved personally in the hostage crisis. On three occasions, I traveled to Iran with other Americans (mostly clergy) in order to meet with government leaders (including the Ayatollah Khomeini, President Bani Sadr, the Foreign Minister, and Speaker of the Parliament), religious leaders, the students occupying the U.S. embassy compound, and others. Our efforts were designed to improve communication and facilitate a nonviolent resolution of the crisis.

On one of these trips, a small group met with then President Bani Sadr. In the course of our conversation, I asked him about the impact of the U.S. embargo, particularly on Iran's military. The former Shah had spent some $20 billion on U.S. weaponry

6. National Council of Churches, "Middle East Policy Statement" (November 5, 1980), pp. 9–10.

between 1973 and 1978. Iran was totally dependent on U.S. weapons and spare parts. I asked President Bani Sadr, "How can your military function without spare parts for F-16s or replacement rounds of ammunition?" Bani Sadr smiled and said:

> We can get anything we need. In spite of the embargo, we are currently doing business with over one hundred American companies. We can get any piece of military hardware we require. We must go through third parties and pay excessively high prices. But, if the money is there, plenty of sellers can be found.

Several years later, another facet of U.S. arms trade with Iran came to light in the startling revelations of the "Iran-Contra" scandal. During the course of prolonged news coverage and Congressional investigations, we learned of schemes and deals about as plausible as most television soap operas: plane loads of sophisticated weapons sent to Iran on instructions from high-ranking White House staff; millions of dollars in "laundered" money changing hands; retired U.S. military personnel, previously unknown multi-millionaire arms brokers and Israeli agents collaborating in the process. While the media predictably focused on whether or not President Reagan and/or then Vice-President Bush knew of these activities, the whole affair revealed volumes about the size and scope of the international arms business. For those who were attentive, the investigation demonstrated just how sophisticated and intricate are the networks and contacts in this lucrative system.

Officially, the government response to the Iran-Contra disclosures was outrage. Several top government officials—including William Casey, Robert McFarlane, Admiral John Poindexter and Oliver North—were dismissed, disgraced and subject to prosecution. The "disgrace" experienced by North and Poindexter was diminished in 1991 when prosecutors dropped criminal proceedings. It seems the damaging testimony they gave to Congress earlier could not be used against them. They eluded prosecution on technicalities, not by dint of innocence. Meanwhile, the White House was remarkably silent. Through it all, little was done to address the underlying problems inherent in the "official" and "unofficial" multi-billion dollar arms industry.

Many people in the churches have argued for years that the profit-driven pattern of global arms sales was both immoral and counter productive. Arming everyone in the Middle East with weapons and then being surprised when military forces use the weapons in ways "we" don't like falls somewhere between hypocritical and naive. I have made this point personally to many legislators and government officials in the U.S. Predictably, most officials deny being hypocritical or naive. Rather, the standard reply is that the arms sales practices were necessary. Their rationale has been reiterated *ad nauseam* in the past: "If we don't sell arms, someone else will!"

The Gulf war and its aftermath have lifted the veil on the Middle East arms bazaar. There is, perhaps, a new day dawning. President Bush included arms control on the post-war agenda during his speech March 6, 1991, to a joint session of the U.S. Congress one week after the formal cessation of the Gulf war. "It would be tragic," Bush said, "if a new arms race were to begin in the Middle East." Later, at the Air Force Academy Commencement, the President spelled out some components of his plan to limit further proliferation of weapons of mass destruction. Selections from his comments reveal the outline of his proposal:

> We are committed to stopping the proliferation of weapons of mass destruction. . . . Halting the proliferation of conventional and unconventional weapons in the Middle East—while supporting the legitimate need of every state to defend itself—will require the cooperation of many states, in the region and around the world. It won't be easy—but the path to peace never is. . . . I am today proposing a Middle East arms control initiative. It features supplier guidelines on conventional arms exports, barriers to exports that contribute to weapons of mass destruction, a freeze now and later a ban on surface-to-surface missiles in the region and a ban on nuclear weapons material.[7]

President Bush also called for a conference of the five leading supplier states—the U.S., the former U.S.S.R., France, Great Britain, and China—to begin setting guidelines on arms sales. Ironically, or perhaps predictably, the world's five main arms suppliers

7. "Bush Unveils Plan for Arms Control in the Middle East," The *New York Times* (May 30, 1991).

are also the permanent members of the United Nations Security Council.

Many hailed the initiative as a much-needed step in the right direction. Other, more skeptical observers quickly pointed out that the gap between rhetoric and reality is profound. Announcing lofty aims without committing the U.S., the "biggest supplier of weapons in the developing world" (the *New York Times*, Aug. 11, 1991), to specific targets left considerable room for maneuver. This caveat, coupled with the fact that the U.S. has continued to pursue major arms sales agreements with various Middle Eastern states in the months after the war, raises serious doubts about the depth of commitment to the stated goals.

James Adams is one such critic. In a penetrating article, "The Arms Trade: The Real Lesson of the Gulf War," Adams acknowledges the Bush Administration's concern with arms control issues. As he traces the behavior of "teams of arms salesmen . . . flocking to the Middle East to tout their wares" just after the war, however, he highlights an important distinction:

> In the wake of the Gulf war the Administration is against these weapons (of mass destruction). It is much less resolutely against the proliferation of weapons of mere destruction, however.[8]

Distinctions among deadly weapons systems are often lost in the rationalizations or what Adams labels the "elastic morality" of day-to-day politics. Much more than high-minded rhetoric will be required if the U.S. and other nations have any real hope of curbing or halting the escalating arms race in the Middle East.

Learning from the Gulf Crisis

The war in the Gulf presented extraordinary dangers to the entire world community. The crisis also provided an opportunity to see systemic problems clearly and the challenge to address them more constructively. We in the United States and people in other nations must learn from this traumatic episode. The multi-

8. James Adams, "The Arms Trade: The Real Lesson of the Gulf War," *Atlantic Monthly* (November, 1991), p.36

faceted issues defy easy resolution. Neither simplistic slogans nor wishful thinking will resolve these daunting problems. Now, more than ever, we must shift from a stimulus/response mode to a proactive one.

The current economic landscape is wholly different than that of ten or twenty years ago. Economic interdependence is a pervasive reality that is here to stay. The dramatic events surrounding the dismantling of the U.S.S.R. and the former socialist states in Eastern Europe in 1990 and 1991 illustrate the point. In the midst of the joy over new freedoms and democratic reforms, these republics face complex economic challenges in the coming decade. Substantial efforts to assist these fledgling democracies grow both from moral and humanitarian concern and from the self-interest of people in other nations. Political and economic stability are concerns that transcend national boundaries. Clearly, their future is linked with our future on this planet of limited resources.

Industrialized and developing nations alike have a pragmatic interest in avoiding crises and oil-related economic shocks like those experienced during the Gulf war. Oil-producing states have various needs as well. Now, in the aftermath of the Gulf war, new, cooperative, multi-national efforts are needed to enhance reserves and insure the steady flow of oil at predictable prices. Organizations such as the European Economic Community (EEC) and the Gulf Cooperation Council (GCC) provide working models for nations committed to pursuing cooperative, multi-national policies. While there are no easy answers, concerted efforts may produce constructive options. The alternative—namely, living with the status quo—is untenable.

Taking responsibility for our consumption is another clear imperative. Major consumer nations must implement measures for conservation. Decreasing our excessive consumption is surely possible and morally necessary. U.S. citizens comprise approximately 5% of the world's population; yet we consume a highly disproportionate amount—perhaps 25%—of the world's resources. The global population now exceeds five billion. Demographers project an additional billion people (or a 20% increase) by the year 2000. The current patterns of consumption will only widen the already staggering gap between the haves and have nots. The deep frustration and resentment born of economic disparity evident in the contemporary Middle East reflects in microcosm the dynamics operative on the world stage. Self-interest and a concern for the larger world community both require substantial changes in the distribution and consumption of the earth's limited resources.

Conservation must also be coupled with vigorous efforts to develop safer, more reliable and renewable sources of energy. Quite apart from the economic and political factors noted above, ecological considerations must weigh heavily in future energy policies. As Daniel Yergin reminds us, various problems are linked with the combustion of fossil fuels—smog and air pollution, depletion of the ozone, and acid rain. Moreover, ecological dangers surround the whole process of producing and transporting oil. Massive oil spills—whether from recklessness, as in the Exxon Valdez spill in Alaska, or deliberate environmental terrorism, as attempted by Saddam Hussein's dumping of crude oil into the Gulf, or setting ablaze more than 700 oil wells in Kuwait—have a long-term impact on the environment. Decreasing dependence on oil is in the long-term interest of all who inhabit this fragile planet.

So, too, do we all have a major stake in halting and reversing the escalating arms race. I have argued in the previous section that the short-term justifications for arms sales and transfers pale in the face of medium- and long-term consequences. International leaders are increasingly audible in their call to stop this profit-driven peddling of sophisticated weapons of mass destruction. It is nothing short of a headlong rush toward catastrophe. Speaking to the House Foreign Affairs Committee during the Gulf war (Feb. 6, 1991), Secretary of State James A. Baker III reflected this view:

> The time has come to try to change the destructive pattern of military competition and proliferation in this region and to reduce the arms flow into an area that is already very over-militarized.

President Bush has echoed this theme and taken the initial steps toward a multi-lateral approach toward arms control. Most authorities agree that a multi-national effort is the only viable way to address the issues. Considerable disagreement exists, even within the U.S. government, on how best to proceed. Some Congressional leaders have offered aggressive and concrete proposals. Lee Hamilton, Chair of the Middle East Subcommittee, for example, advocated the following before his colleagues on the House Foreign Affairs Committee on March 20, 1991:

> I would recommend a unilateral pause in the sale of arms for a limited period of time—a few months—during which we would work to develop an international consortium of the principal arms sellers to see if we can develop a regime to limit the flow of arms to the Middle East.

Whatever the outcome of President Bush's post-war initiative, it has served to put critical issues out on the table. The established patterns of arms sales and transfers are obviously unwise for pragmatic reasons; many would argue that the whole process is morally indefensible. Concerned citizens, particularly those living in countries that produce and sell the armaments, must seize this moment. We must monitor what is happening in our lands and what is being said and done by government officials. We must ask hard questions as we sort through information that confuses image with reality. We must recognize that we are part of the problem. If the dangerous proliferation of weapons and technologies continues, we will all be the victims of the conflagrations.

There is no doubt that we live in a dangerous world where confusing issues converge in volatile ways. Nowhere is this more evident than in the contemporary Middle East. For people of faith, war is not the answer. There is a better, though not an easier way in a ministry of reconciliation.

The crisis in the Gulf has provided a window through which we can see more clearly some of the issues—religious, political, and economic—confronting all who share this planet. The challenge is to look through that window, to learn from these unsettling events and to reshape attitudes and actions in an effort to fashion a more hopeful future. We cannot change what has already happened. But we do bear a responsibility for what happens next.

RESOURCES FOR FURTHER READING

Islam and Middle Eastern Religious Communities

Angle of Vision: Christians and the Middle East, by Charles A. Kimball (New York: Friendship Press, 1992). An ecumenical study that explores the contemporary challenges and opportunities for North American and Middle Eastern Christians in their common concern for Christian witness and responsible citizenship.

Faith & Power: The Politics of Islam, by Edward Mortimer (New York: Random House, 1982). Presents a well-informed British journalist's engaging account of Islamic forces in the midst of political changes in several countries. Slightly dated, but useful background information.

For the Land and the Lord: Jewish Fundamentalism in Israel, by Ian S. Lustick (New York: Council on Foreign Relations, 1988). A careful, scholarly, and engaging study of the religious and political ideology and tactics of a powerful segment within Israel.

A History of the Jews, by Paul Johnson (New York: Harper and Row, 1987). A compressed, but well-written overview of Jewish history from the time of the ancient Israelites to the modern state of Israel.

Islam: The Straight Path, by John L. Esposito (New York: Oxford University Press, rev. ed., 1990). An excellent introduction to Islam with particular emphasis on the resurgence of Islam during the past two centuries.

Prophecy and Politics: The Secret Alliance Between Israel and the U.S. Christian Right, by Grace Halsell (Chicago: Lawrence Hill Books, rev. ed., 1986). A provocative exploration of the religious and political worldviews and contemporary machinations of a major segment of the American Christian community.

Sacred Rage: The Crusade of Modern Islam, by Robin Wright (New York: Simon & Schuster, 1985). A seasoned journalist surveys and explains Islamic movements in several Middle Eastern countries.

Striving Together: A Way Forward in Christian-Muslim Relations, by Charles A. Kimball (Maryknoll, NY: Orbis Books, 1991). An introduction to Islam and the problems plaguing Christian-Muslim relations. This book examines the practical and theological isues in an effort to discover a way forward for the adherents in the world's two largest religious communities.

The Wrath of Jonah: The Crisis of Religious Nationalism in the Israeli-Palestinian Conflict, by Rosemary R. and Herman J. Ruether (San Francisco: Harper and Row, 1989). A controversial analysis of biblical, theological, and political issues that have arisen over the centuries as different religious communites have claimed the same land. The focus is on the moral and political dilemmas facing Israel today.

Middle Eastern Politics

Arab and Jew: Wounded Spirits in a Promised Land, by David K. Shipler (New York: Times Books, 1986). A thoughtful and compassionate book that moves beyond details in order to put a human face on those caught in the ongoing conflict. Shipler, a former *New York Times* bureau chief in Jerusalem, won a Pulitzer Prize for this book in 1987.

From Beirut to Jerusalem, by Thomas Friedman (New York: Farrar, Straus, & Giroux Inc., 1989). A powerful, no-holds-barred assessment of the political machinations operative in Lebanon, Syria, and Israel. Friedman, a two-time Pulitzer Prize winner who spent a decade in Beirut and Jerusalem as bureau chief for the *New York*

Times, weaves spirited commentary, humor, and a sharp critique of all parties throughout this book.

Beyond Innocence and Redemption: Confronting the Holocaust and Israeli Power, by Marc H. Ellis (San Francisco: Harper and Row, 1990). A provocative critique of militant Zionism by a Jewish scholar. Ellis argues that Martin Buber, Hannah Arendt, and others provide the key insights to guide Jewish people toward a more just and secure future.

The Blood of Abraham: Insights into the Middle East, by Jimmy Carter (Boston: Houghton Mifflin Co., 1985). An assessment of the religious and historical perspectives as well as the contemporary issues facing the decendants of Abraham.

A Compassionate Peace: A Future for Israel, Palestine, and the Middle East, by Everett Mendelsohn (New York: Hill and Wang, rev. ed., 1989). Perhaps the single best one-volume introduction to the major issues converging in the Middle East. This text, prepared under the auspices of the American Friends Service Committee, combines thoughtful analysis with realistic and hopeful alternatives for a more peaceful and just future.

A History of the Arab Peoples, by Albert Hourani (Cambridge, MA: Harvard University Press, 1991). A well-written, scholarly history of the Arabs from the rise of Islam to the present day.

A Peace to End All Peace: The Fall of the Ottoman Empire and the Creation of the Modern Middle East, by David Fromkin (New York: Avon Books, 1989). A reliable guide through the multi-sided external and internal political developments that have shaped the Middle East in this century.

Republic of Fear: The Politics of Modern Iraq, by Samir al-Khalil (Berkeley: University of California Press, 1989). A compelling and chilling assessment of the apparatus of state terror developed and implemented under the rule of Saddam Hussein.

Saddam Hussein and the Crisis in the Gulf, by Judith Miller and Laurie Mylroie (New York: Times Books, 1990). This "instant" book by two knowledgeable Middle East specialists spells out the background and context for Iraq's 1990 invasion of Kuwait. The assessment of Saddam Hussein's pre-1990 "special" relationship with Washington is particularly helpful.

Winning the War, Losing Our Souls, by James M. Wall (Chicago: Christian Century Press, 1991). An insightful and provocative collection of twenty-one editorials published in *The Christian Century* between June 1990 and June 1991.

Oil, Arms, and Economic Interdependence in the Middle East

Arms and Oil: U.S. Military Strategy and the Persian Gulf, by Thomas L. McNaugher (Washington: The Brookings Institution, 1985). Written from the perspective of perceived U.S. interests, this text provides a straightforward analysis of the operative issues in the Gulf as well as a strategy for developing a broad-based approach to "security."

The Control of the Middle East Arms Race, by Geoffrey Kemp (Washington, D.C.: Carnegie Endowment for International Peace, 1991). A sobering overview of arms production, procurement, and transfers in the Middle East today. The author, who served on the National Security Council Staff and in the Department of Defense, argues for "realistic" arms control based on progress in resolving regional conflicts.

The Global Politics of Arms Sales, by Andrew J. Pierre (Princeton: Princeton University Press, 1982). Produced under the auspices of the Council of Foreign Relations, this book examines the incentives, dilemmas, and restraints confronting suppliers and recipients of modern weapons.

The Prize: The Epic Quest for Oil, Money and Power, by Daniel Yergin (New York: Simon & Schuster, 1991). A powerful, insightful, and unsettling narrative history of black gold, "the prize." This massive, yet readable book includes extensive notes and bibliographical information to point the interested reader toward numerous books and articles.